I0456920

CALLED
to Serve
The Braver With Belief Guided Journal

Called to Serve
Published by Authentically Created
PO Box 532
Springboro, Ohio 45066
www.authenticallycreated.com

Authentically Created is a division of Lilian Grace Designs, LLC

ISBN 979-8-9898545-6-1 (paperback)

Cover art and interior by Shonda Ramsey

Printed in the United States of America
First Edition 2025

10 9 8 7 6 5 4 3 2 1

091625

For all who feel called to serve.

Have hope, for one day you'll soon have the confidence needed to boldly lead. I pray that throughout these pages you'll learn how to be brave as you enter the incredible life of servant leadership. You are called to serve.

Contents

Introduction

To boldly lead where I felt God calling me, I had to first undergo a season of refinement. Preparing to lead in love was important to me—I knew I had to establish a plan. This *Called to Serve Guided Journal* provides you with prompts to help you build your plan to lead in love. It's a valuable tool to work through the thoughts and emotions you have, discover limiting beliefs you need to conquer, and helps instill confidence that you are *called to serve* by God.

What you can expect for each chapter:

Choose Your Target: Keep things simple and reduce the chance for overthrow. This section helps you pick one target to focus on each chapter and knock down the barriers in your way.

Raise Your Bow: You cannot shoot an arrow without a bow. This section helps you keep a list of tools and resources needed to help you hit your target.

The Draw: Like pulling the bowstring back, this section takes a closer look at a few highlights from each chapter and the deeper lessons they hold.

Centered Aim: If you want to hit the bullseye, you must center your aim. This section recaps the chapter's scripture and prayer.

Follow Through: To prevent premature dropping of the bow arm, a strong archer maintains their form after release. This section is a space for you to plan and track your steps.

Resources to Have on Hand

This is an interactive book, with encouragement to act on refining your heart and preparing to lead. There are resources listed here that I personally use daily; they will help you maximize your experience. I recommend gathering as many of these items as possible and putting them in a tote bag or some other small mobile container so you can take them wherever you choose to do each activity. I call this my growth bag.

Growth Bag Contents:

- Braver with Belief Book
- Called to Serve Guided Journal
- Pocket or digital Bible
    - YouVersion App (or other similar)
- Journal
- Pens
- Paper (loose)
- Colored pencils, markers, or crayons
- Mirror
- Sticky notes or a dry erase marker
- Spotify Playlist

A Curated Spotify Playlist that coordinates with *Braver with Belief*

All that stands between you and becoming braver with belief is an open heart and mind. I ask that you give yourself grace and patience as you work through some difficult exercises to get to the root of what God is asking you to let go of to prepare your heart for becoming a servant leader.

Friend, I know this feels scary. You may be afraid and feel alone in your desire to answer the calling God has placed on your heart to become a leader. I know this because I am right there beside you. You aren't alone; God wants you to know He has prepared and equipped you for a time such as this. You have what it takes to be a leader. You just need to refine your heart a bit to help you confidently lead.

I hope that by sharing with you my innermost thoughts and fears, you will come to know and understand that while I may not be able to fully understand your experiences and expertise, I can empathize. Will you join me as we boldly step out in faith and with a resounding yes, fulfill the calling God has placed on our hearts?

Dedication

I, _____, commit to not only reading 'Braver with Belief' but also promise to open my heart as I engage with and apply the journal prompts and exercises provided at the end of each chapter and throughout this journal as I begin to refine my heart and confidently step into the role of servant leadership.

Signed,   Date:_____

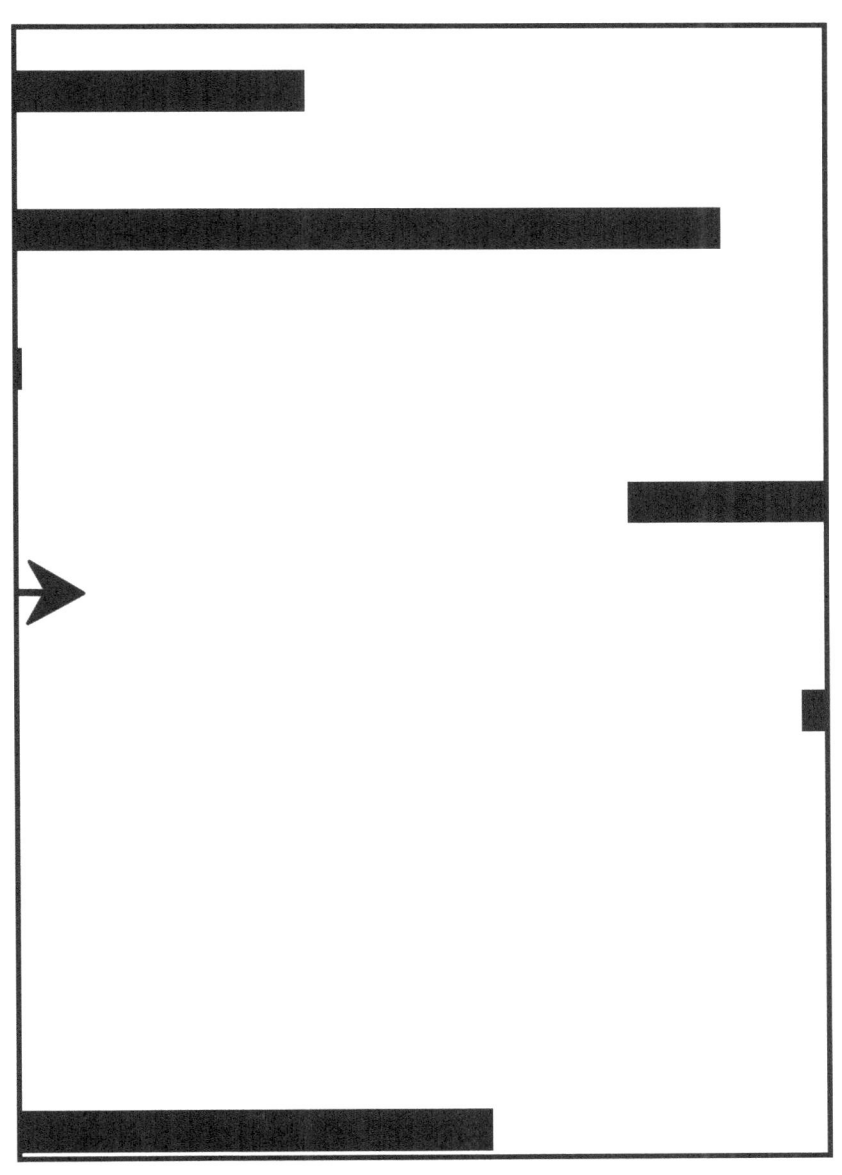

Chapter one

-

Unexpected Circumstances

Most unexpected circumstances are beyond our control, which can induce fear and anxiety as we struggle to regain a sense of control in the situation. Our insistent need to be in charge of our own outcomes drives us to cling on a bit too tightly to most situations. Letting go of the desire to control these situations and allow your faith to override your fear will restore your hope.

Choose Your Target: Keep things simple and reduce the chance for overthrow. This section helps you pick one target to focus on each chapter and knock down the barriers in your way.

Think back to a time when you weathered a storm unexpectedly.

What event led to the hardship?

_____

_____

_____

_____

_____

_____

_____

How did you react/respond?

_____

_____

_____

_____

_____

_____

_____

How do you wish you had reacted/responded?

_____

_____

_____

_____

_____

_____

_____

What did you learn through this difficult time? *List everything that comes to mind.*

_____
_____
_____
_____
_____
_____
_____
_____
_____
_____
_____
_____
_____

What do you need to let go of from this lesson?

_____
_____
_____
_____

What are three key takeaways from this storm?

1 _____
2 _____
3 _____

What one lesson from this storm can you use to teach others?

_____
_____
_____

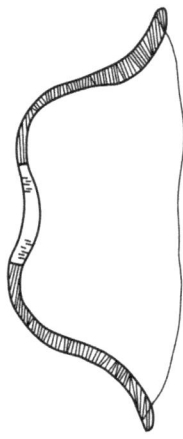

Raise Your Bow: You cannot shoot an arrow without a bow. This section helps you keep a list of tools and resources needed to help you hit your target.

Keep in mind the one lesson from this storm you can use to teach others. What tools or resources do you need to teach someone else from your experience?

_____
_____
_____
_____
_____
_____
_____
_____
_____
_____
_____
_____

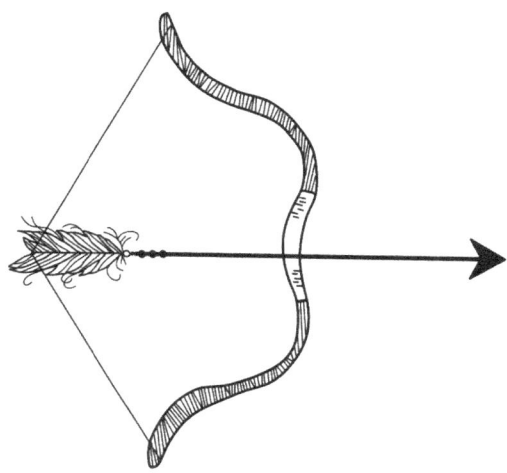

The Draw: Like pulling the bowstring back, this section takes a closer look at each chapter's highlights and the deeper lessons they hold.

Making your faith a priority will serve you well as you seek God's help in becoming braver with belief.

What has stopped you from making faith a priority?

_____

_____

_____

_____

_____

How can you make faith a priority now?

_____

_____

_____

_____

_____

List out an ideal schedule to include faith in your daily/weekly/monthly plan.

_____
_____
_____
_____
_____

Nothing swept away matters.

What are you holding onto too tightly because you are afraid of letting it go?

_____
_____
_____
_____
_____

What is stopping you from answering your calling?

_____
_____
_____
_____
_____

What do you need to sweep away to clear the path for something new?

_____
_____
_____
_____
_____

Centered Aim: If you want to hit the bullseye, center your aim. This section recaps the chapter's scripture and prayer.

> *"For our light and momentary troubles are achieving for us an eternal glory that far outweighs them all. So we fix our eyes not on what is seen, but on what is unseen, since what is seen is temporary, but what is unseen is eternal."*
>   2 Corinthians 4:17-18

> *"Cast all your anxiety on him because he cares for you."*
>   1 Peter 5:7

Prayer:
> *Father, I am so sorry that I took my eyes off of you. Help me release my constant need to control everything I do and allow you the chance to lead me where you want. Please forgive me for focusing on the things that I can see and not trusting your guidance. Amen.*

Follow Through: To prevent premature dropping of the bow arm, a strong archer maintains their form after release. This section is a space for you to plan and track your steps.

How will you teach others the lesson learned during your unexpected circumstance?

_____

_____

_____

_____

_____

_____

_____

_____

_____

_____

_____

_____

_____

What steps do you need to take to start now?

_____

_____

_____

_____

_____

_____

_____

_____

_____

_____

_____

_____

_____

_____

_____

_____

_____

_____

_____

What is the deadline to complete this?

_____

_____

_____

After completing this section, add the steps needed as tasks in your to-do list.
Set important dates and reminders to stay on target for your deadline date.

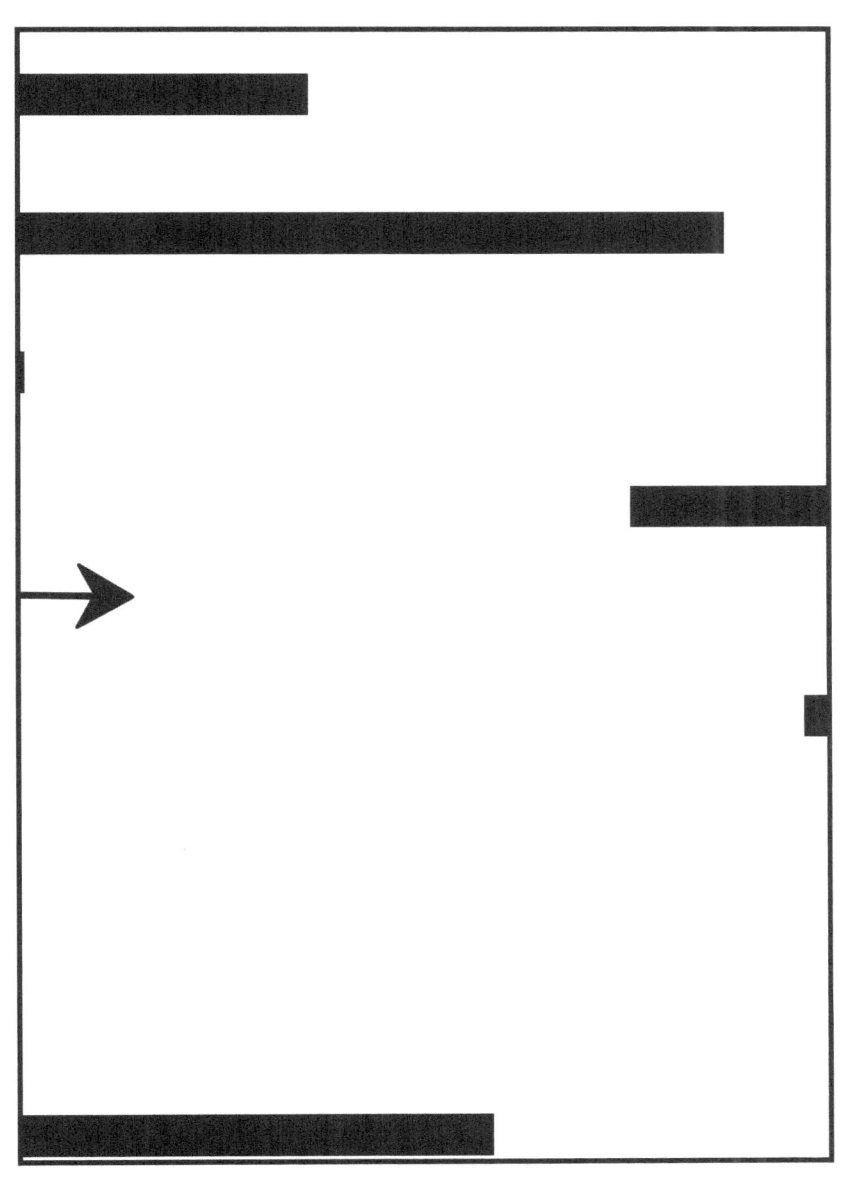

chapter Two

Letting Go of Grudges

Even if life for you doesn't bring forth children—or any other thing you feel is missing—*your life still matters.* There are extremely fulfilling things you can do outside of what you envisioned. This doesn't mean the grief of this loss goes away. It will always be there, but it means that you can choose to live life again as you give birth to many new ideas with God's guidance.

Choose Your Target: Keep things simple and reduce the chance for overthrow. This section helps you pick one target to focus on each chapter and knock down the barriers in your way.

Invite God to join you as you brainstorm new ideas to fulfill the desire you have or had at some time to be a servant leader. Write down every thought you have.

_____

_____

_____

_____

_____

_____

_____

_____

_____

_____

_____

_____

_____

_____

_____

_____

_____

_____

_____

_____

_____

_____

_____

_____

_____

_____

_____

Reviewing your list, put a star next to ten that really stand out to you.

Consider the ten stars. Circle the ones you've been apprehensive to complete because of something that was said to you, causing you to doubt. List up to five of them here.

_____

_____

_____

_____

_____

From your list of five, highlight the top three you desire to fulfill the most.

1 _____

2 _____

3 _____

Which one of those three can you work towards right now?

_____

_____

_____

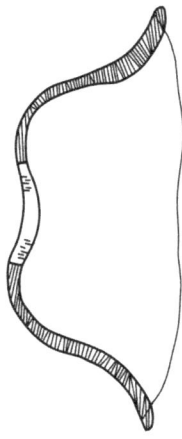

Raise Your Bow: You cannot shoot an arrow without a bow. This section helps you keep a list of tools and resources needed to help you hit your target.

Keep in mind the one new idea you want to start work on now. What tools or resources do you need to begin working on and implementing this idea?

_____

_____

_____

_____

_____

_____

_____

_____

_____

_____

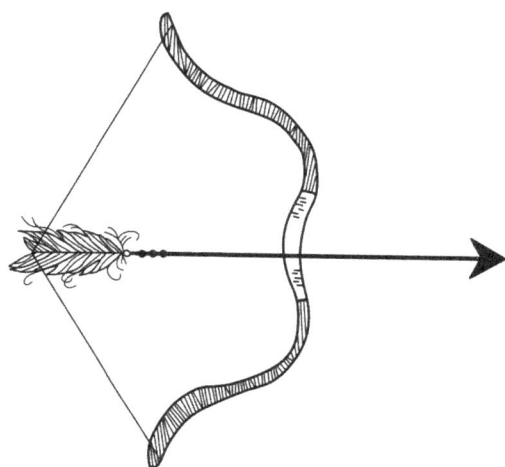

The Draw: Like pulling the bowstring back, this section takes a closer look at each chapter's highlights and the deeper lessons they hold.

By changing how you approach your friendships, you are actively working on a better way to handle conflict with others. With time, you'll strengthen your communication skills, which will help you become a stronger leader.

Have you experienced conflict with others?

_____

_____

_____

What do you wish you would have done differently in your approach to the conflict?

_____

_____

_____

_____

Letting Go of Grudges | 29

What is something you can do to strengthen your communication skills as a whole?

_____

_____

_____

_____

_____

_____

_____

Don't let jealousy consume you when others receive the blessings you crave. Focus on you and your relationship with God during this season of your life.

How can you better identify and stop a jealous spirit bubbling up inside of you?

_____

_____

_____

_____

_____

_____

_____

Choose a Bible verse to help you redirect your jealousy. Write it here:

_____

_____

_____

_____

_____

_____

Write a letter to God with an admission of your struggle to let go of grudges and moments of jealousy.

My loving Father,

_____
_____
_____
_____
_____
_____
_____
_____
_____
_____
_____
_____
_____
_____
_____
_____
_____

All my love,

Seek forgiveness in prayer.
Write down how this exercise made you feel.

_____
_____
_____
_____
_____

Centered Aim: If you want to hit the bullseye, center your aim. This section recaps the chapter's scripture and prayer.

> *"Whoever would foster love covers over an offense, but whoever repeats the matter separates close friends."*
>
> Proverbs 17:9

> *"And when you stand praying, if you hold anything against anyone, forgive them, so that your Father in heaven may forgive you your sins."*
>
> Mark 11:25

Prayer:

> *Father, I am so sorry I didn't respond in love. Help me let go of the bitterness I harbor against others out of jealousy. Please forgive me for allowing grudges to take root and separate me from my close friends. Amen.*

Follow Through: To prevent premature dropping of the bow arm, a strong archer maintains their form after release. This section is a space for you to plan and track your steps.

It's time to let go of hurt feelings and grudges held towards the person who caused you to stop fulfilling your original idea(s).

_____

_____

_____

How will you bravely begin leading in the area you chose from your list?

_____

_____

_____

_____

_____

_____

_____

What steps do you need to take to start now?

_____

_____

_____

_____

_____

_____

_____

_____

_____

_____

_____

_____

_____

_____

_____

_____

_____

_____

_____

_____

_____

What is the deadline to complete this?

_____

_____

_____

After completing this section, add the steps needed as tasks in your to-do list. Set important dates and reminders to stay on target for your deadline date.

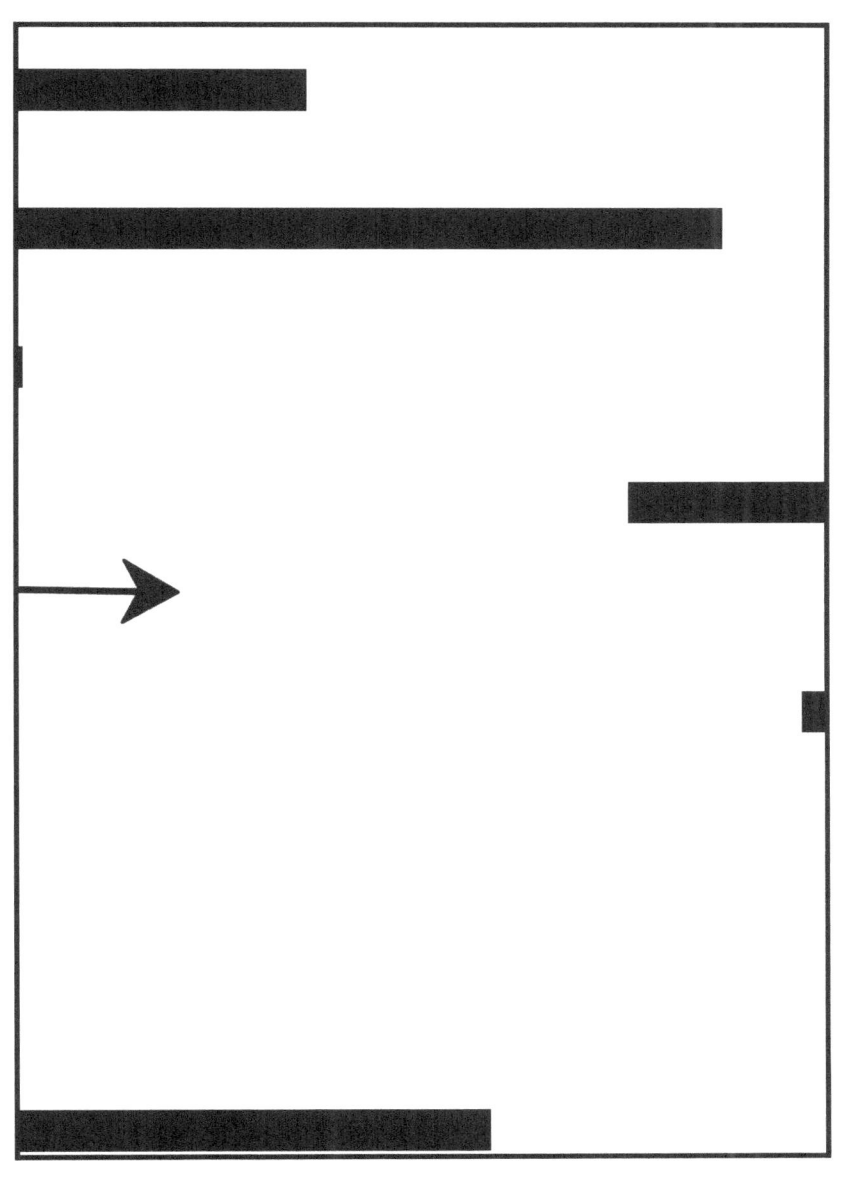

chapter Three

Overcoming Regret

Being brave enough to initiate change in your life is admirable. Seek God's direction, wisdom, and patience as you put a new plan in place to work on you. Be honest with family and friends about what you are working towards and firm when you say no to things that will slow your progress. You'll find that they'll likely encourage you more than they'll discourage you. You are doing a great job so far!

Choose Your Target: Keep things simple and reduce the chance for overthrow. This section helps you pick one target to focus on each chapter and knock down the barriers in your way.

Consider something you have regretted not doing throughout your lifetime. It could be a business goal, a lifestyle change, or a dream you once had.

_____

_____

_____

_____

Write out an alternative outcome as if you've already done it. What would it look like to achieve this goal?

_____

_____

_____

_____

_____

What defining steps would you have needed to take to reach this alternative outcome successfully?

_____

_____

_____

_____

_____

_____

_____

_____

_____

_____

_____

What stopped you from taking these steps before?

_____

_____

_____

_____

_____

_____

_____

_____

_____

_____

Pick three steps that feel more achievable to you right now.

1 _____

2 _____

3 _____

Pick one of these three steps to begin working towards now.

_____

_____

_____

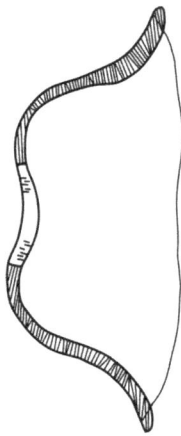

Raise Your Bow: You cannot shoot an arrow without a bow. This section helps you keep a list of tools and resources needed to help you hit your target.

Keep in mind the one achievable step. What tools or resources do you need to begin working on to fulfill this one goal?

_____

_____

_____

_____

_____

_____

_____

_____

_____

_____

_____

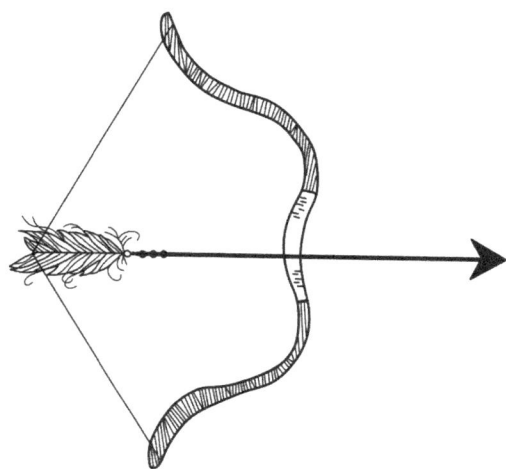

The Draw: Like pulling the bowstring back, this section takes a closer look at each chapter's highlights and the deeper lessons they hold.

Recognizing the need for more gentleness and realistic self-expectations, I find myself in a new place: my goal isn't to have a perfect body, but a healthy one that will help me serve others for a long time.

What expectations have you been placing upon yourself?

_____

_____

_____

_____

_____

_____

_____

_____

_____

How can you have a more gentle approach with your self-expectations?

_____
_____
_____
_____
_____

What does it mean to have realistic self-expectations for your situation?

_____
_____
_____
_____
_____

Be only in competition with who you were yesterday as you work towards becoming a better version of yourself today.

Why do you feel a desire to be in competition with others?

_____
_____
_____
_____
_____

How can you overcome the desire to be the one to win?

_____
_____
_____
_____
_____

What is one mindset shift you can make to redirect your competitive nature to be more focused on being a better version of yourself today than who you were yesterday?

_____

_____

_____

_____

_____

When you overcome the regret you harbor, you are free to move forward into all that God has waiting for you.

What do you believe God has waiting for you?

_____

_____

_____

_____

_____

How does it feel to be able to freely move forward?

_____

_____

_____

_____

_____

How can you guard your heart against regret in the future?

_____

_____

_____

_____

Centered Aim: If you want to hit the bullseye, center your aim. This section recaps the chapter's scripture and prayer.

"Forget the former things; do not dwell on the past. See, I am doing a new thing! Now it springs up; do you not perceive it? I am making a way in the wilderness and streams in the wasteland."
Isaiah 43:18-19

"Godly sorrow brings repentance that leads to salvation and leaves no regret, but worldly sorrow brings death."
2 Corinthians 7:10

Prayer:
Father, I am so sorry I have been carrying around regret for so long. Help me let go of regret as I work on bettering myself. Please forgive me for negatively speaking to myself as I struggled to face my past mistakes. Amen.

Follow Through: To prevent premature dropping of the bow arm, a strong archer maintains their form after release. This section is a space for you to plan and track your steps.

We are no longer carrying regret with us. How will you begin working towards taking the first step towards the goal you've been putting off?

_____

_____

_____

_____

_____

_____

_____

_____

_____

_____

_____

_____

_____

_____

What steps do you need to take to start now?

_____

_____

_____

_____

_____

_____

_____

_____

_____

_____

_____

_____

_____

_____

_____

_____

_____

_____

_____

_____

What is the deadline to complete this?

_____

_____

_____

After completing this section, add the steps needed as tasks in your to-do list. Set important dates and reminders to stay on target for your deadline date.

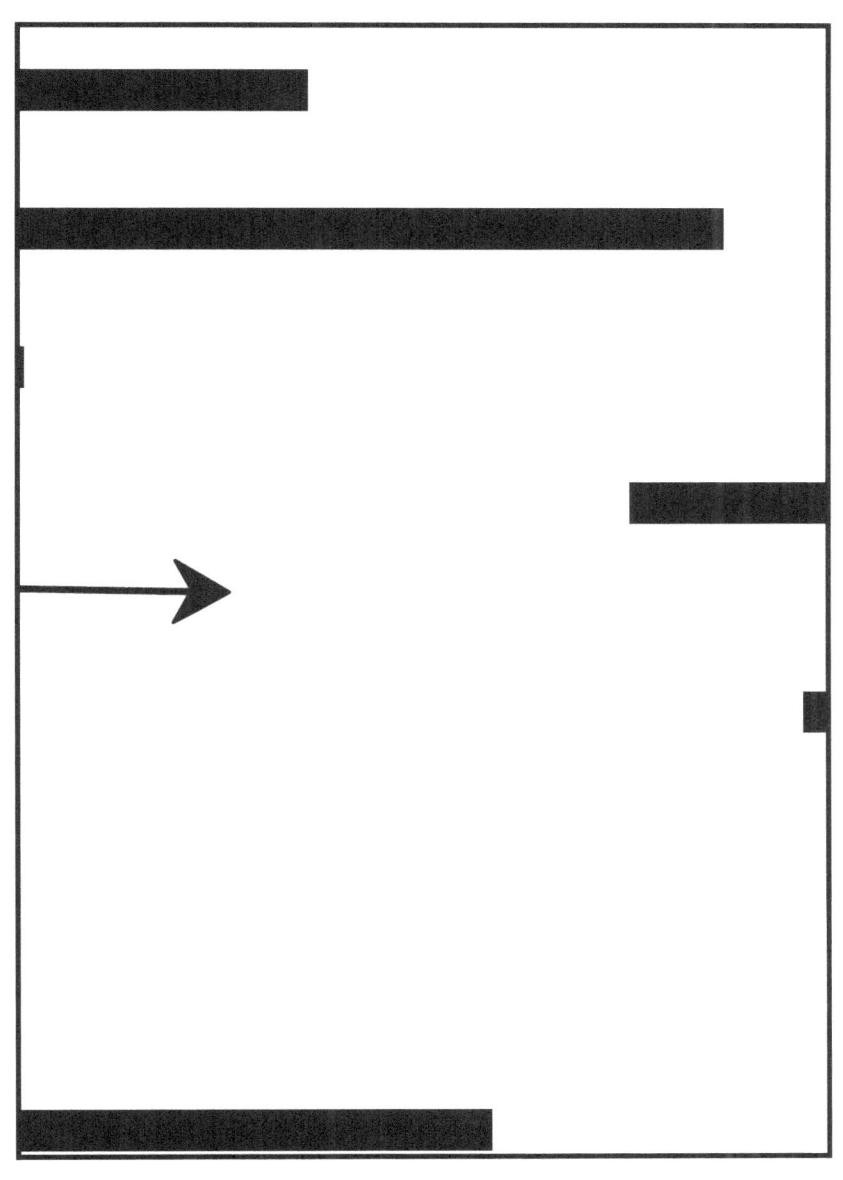

Chapter Four

Path to Forgiveness

Extending Forgiveness towards yourself allows you the chance to be free from the shame and guilt you carry. Redemption is found with forgiveness. Once you have walked through forgiveness, do not dwell on it any longer. Remember to check in with yourself often. Don't let the enemy distract you from God's calling on your life by trying to convince you that you aren't the right person to lead His flock. As you ask God for forgiveness of your wrongdoings, you should also extend forgiveness to yourself.

Choose Your Target: Keep things simple and reduce the chance for overthrow. This section helps you pick one target to focus on each chapter and knock down the barriers in your way.

This exercise may be difficult and emotional to do. Allow time to work through it and give yourself grace to process fully what this exercise brings to the surface.

Make a list of all the things you feel disqualify you from being a servant leader. Include an explanation with each item you write.

For example, one of mine is negative self-talk. I genuinely don't want to be miserable all the time, yet sometimes I can't help but scold myself for something I did or said that made me question it later.

_____
_____
_____
_____
_____
_____
_____
_____
_____
_____
_____
_____
_____
_____
_____
_____
_____
_____
_____
_____
_____

Looking back at your list, categorize it into skillset and mindset. For example, if it is something you can learn, that would be considered a skill set. If it is something you have to work on mentally, this would be mindset work. Indicate each category by writing either the letter "s" or "m" next to it.

From your mindset list, circle the three areas you struggle with the most. Write them here.

1 _____

2 _____

3 _____

From the three you circled, pick one to conquer now.

_____

_____

_____

Check in: Take some time to process your feelings after this exercise.

_____

_____

_____

_____

_____

_____

_____

_____

_____

_____

_____

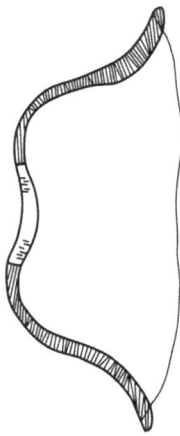

Raise Your Bow: You cannot shoot an arrow without a bow. This section helps you keep a list of tools and resources needed to help you hit your target.

Keep in mind the one mindset shift you can make now. What tools or resources do you need to begin working on forgiving yourself and improving upon this limiting belief?

_____

_____

_____

_____

_____

_____

_____

_____

_____

_____

_____

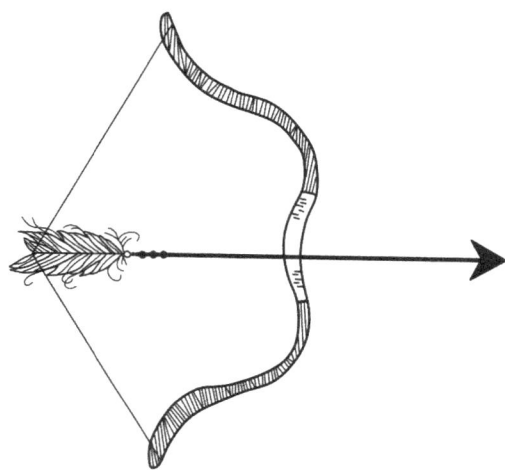

The Draw: Like pulling the bowstring back, this section takes a closer look at each chapter's highlights and the deeper lessons they hold.

Because I had conquered one of the hardest things yet—forgiving myself—I knew I would succeed.

What does succeeding mean to you?

_____

_____

_____

Why do you feel it's difficult for you to forgive yourself?

_____

_____

_____

_____

_____

_____

What does conquering these limiting beliefs instill in your heart?

_____

_____

_____

_____

_____

Negative self-talk, I believe, was the enemy's tool to keep me mentally captive.

What forms of negative self-talk do you often do?

_____

_____

_____

_____

_____

What truth can breathe into these areas? Include scripture references.

_____

_____

_____

_____

_____

What one phrase or thought can you memorize to help shift your negative self-talk the moment it happens?

_____

_____

_____

_____

Centered Aim: If you want to hit the bullseye, center your aim. This section recaps the chapter's scripture and prayer.

"'Come now, let us settle the matter,' says the LORD. 'Though your sins are like scarlet, they shall be as white as snow; though they are red as crimson, they shall be like wool.'"
Isaiah 1:18

"Therefore, I tell you, her many sins have been forgiven—as her great love has shown. But whoever has been forgiven little loves little."
Luke 7:47

Prayer:
Father, I apologize for being unkind to myself. Help me let go of negative self-talk as I work on becoming a more positive person. Please forgive me for not being kinder to my temple. Amen.

Follow Through: To prevent premature dropping of the bow arm, a strong archer maintains their form after release. This section is a space for you to plan and track your steps.

We are no longer believing we are unqualified. God qualifies those who He calls, and that includes you. What do you need to do right now to forgive yourself and begin improving your mindset?

_____

_____

_____

_____

_____

_____

_____

_____

_____

_____

_____

_____

What steps do you need to take to start now?

_____
_____
_____
_____
_____
_____
_____
_____
_____
_____
_____
_____
_____
_____
_____
_____
_____
_____
_____
_____
_____

What is the deadline to complete this?

_____
_____
_____

After completing this section, add the steps needed as tasks in your to-do list. Set important dates and reminders to stay on target for your deadline date.

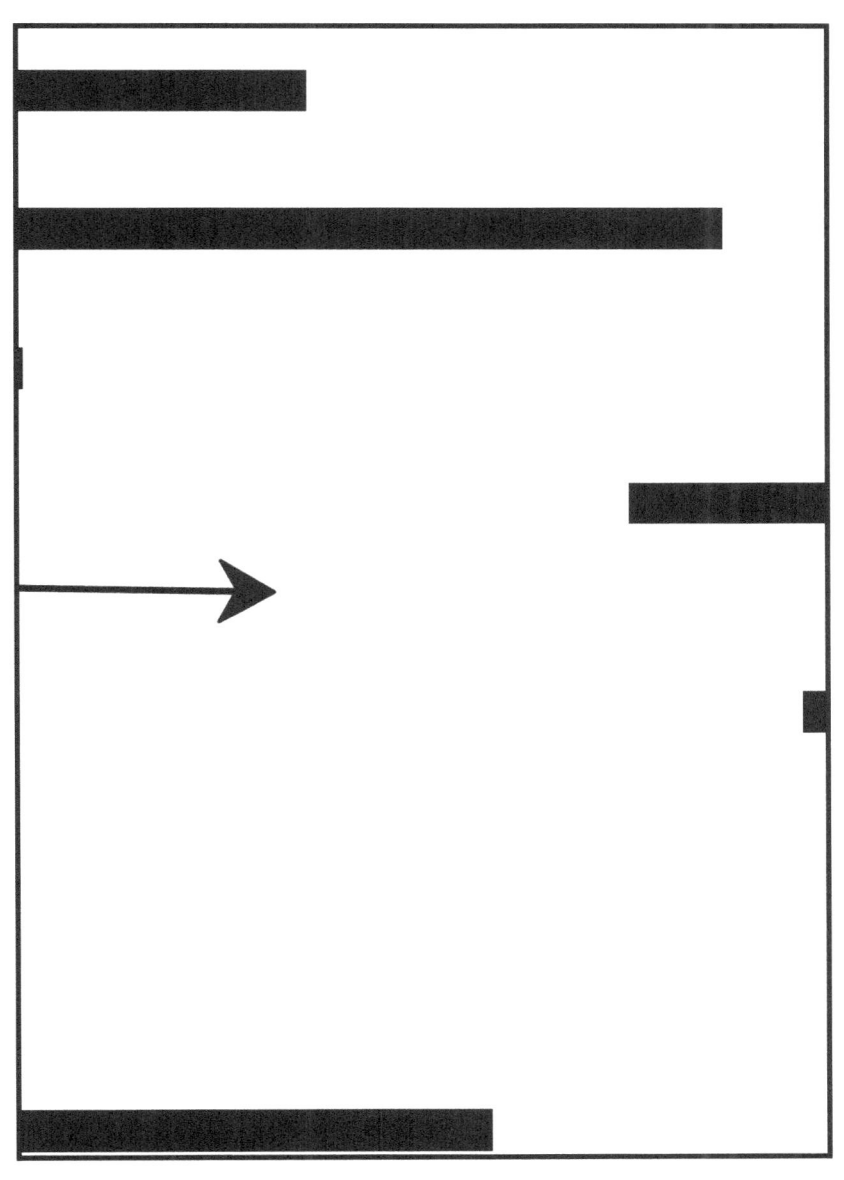

Chapter Five

Mending Past Hurts

Relax your shoulders, release the grip on your jaw, and breathe in through your nose and out through your mouth. I want to challenge you to recognize the need to do this exercise during moments of stress. The more you do it, the more peace you allow to enter, which helps you move forward with hope—and without carrying the hurt you feel.

Choose Your Target: Keep things simple and reduce the chance for overthrow. This section helps you pick one target to focus on each chapter and knock down the barriers in your way.

This exercise may be difficult and emotional to do. Allow time to work through it and give yourself grace to process fully what this exercise brings to surface

Make a timeline of things that happened to you, shaping who you are today.

Date	Event

Reflecting on your timeline, put a star next to up to eight pivotal things that resulted in hurt or painful memories. From the eight, list the key five that still have significant influence.

_____

_____

_____

_____

_____

Of the five moments, choose three that you have mended, and feel would be impactful teachable moments to help someone else in a similar situation.

1_____

2_____

3_____

Which one moment could you confidently begin teaching right now?

_____

_____

_____

Check in: Take some time to process your feelings after this exercise.

_____

_____

_____

_____

_____

_____

_____

_____

Mending Past Hurts   63

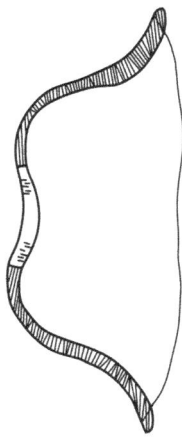

Raise Your Bow: You cannot shoot an arrow without a bow. This section helps you keep a list of tools and resources needed to help you hit your target.

Keep in mind the one moment you feel confident in teaching now. What tools or resources do you need to build your lesson on this topic? Is it a course, a book, or a presentation you could give? Define it.

_____

_____

_____

_____

_____

_____

_____

_____

_____

_____

_____

_____

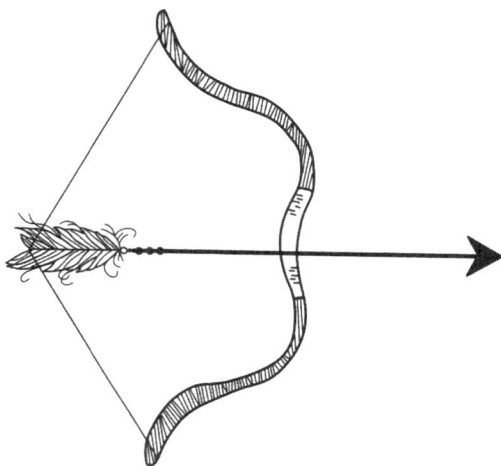

The Draw: Like pulling the bowstring back, this section takes a closer look at each chapter's highlights and the deeper lessons they hold.

I didn't discover peace and joy until I returned to a life that put God first every single day.

Identify areas in your daily life where there may be missed moments spent with God.

_____

_____

_____

_____

What can you change within your daily schedule to prioritize time with God first?

_____

_____

_____

What do you hope to achieve by spending more time with God first daily?

_____

_____

_____

_____

Life may still be difficult, but because I have done the hard work of mending my past hurts, I feel better equipped to face whatever comes my way with God by my side.

Reflecting on your timeline, what past hurts still need mending?

_____

_____

_____

_____

_____

What are some things you can do to start mending those areas?

_____

_____

_____

_____

_____

What does mending your past hurts mean to you?

_____

_____

_____

_____

_____

Centered Aim: If you want to hit the bullseye, center your aim. This section recaps the chapter's scripture and prayer.

> *"But I will restore you to health and heal your wounds,' declares the LORD, 'because you are called an outcast, Zion for whom no one cares.'"*
>
> Jeremiah 30:17

> *"The LORD is close to the brokenhearted and saves those who are crushed in spirit."*
>
> Psalm 34:18

Prayer:

> *Father, I am so sorry that I have been trying to carry the weight of my past hurts on my shoulders alone. Help me let go of the need to withstand the pain as I invite you to sit with me in my pain. Please forgive me for allowing this pain to cause additional stress in my life and not working towards mending it sooner. Amen.*

Follow Through: To prevent premature dropping of the bow arm, a strong archer maintains their form after release. This section is a space for you to plan and track your steps.

What changes in your schedule do you need to make to prioritize this one lesson you want to share with others?

_____

_____

_____

_____

_____

_____

_____

_____

_____

_____

_____

_____

_____

What steps do you need to take to start now?

_____

_____

_____

_____

_____

_____

_____

_____

_____

_____

_____

_____

_____

_____

_____

_____

_____

_____

_____

_____

What is the deadline to complete this?

_____

_____

_____

After completing this section, add the steps needed as tasks in your to-do list. Set important dates and reminders to stay on target for your deadline date.

Mending Past Hurts | 69

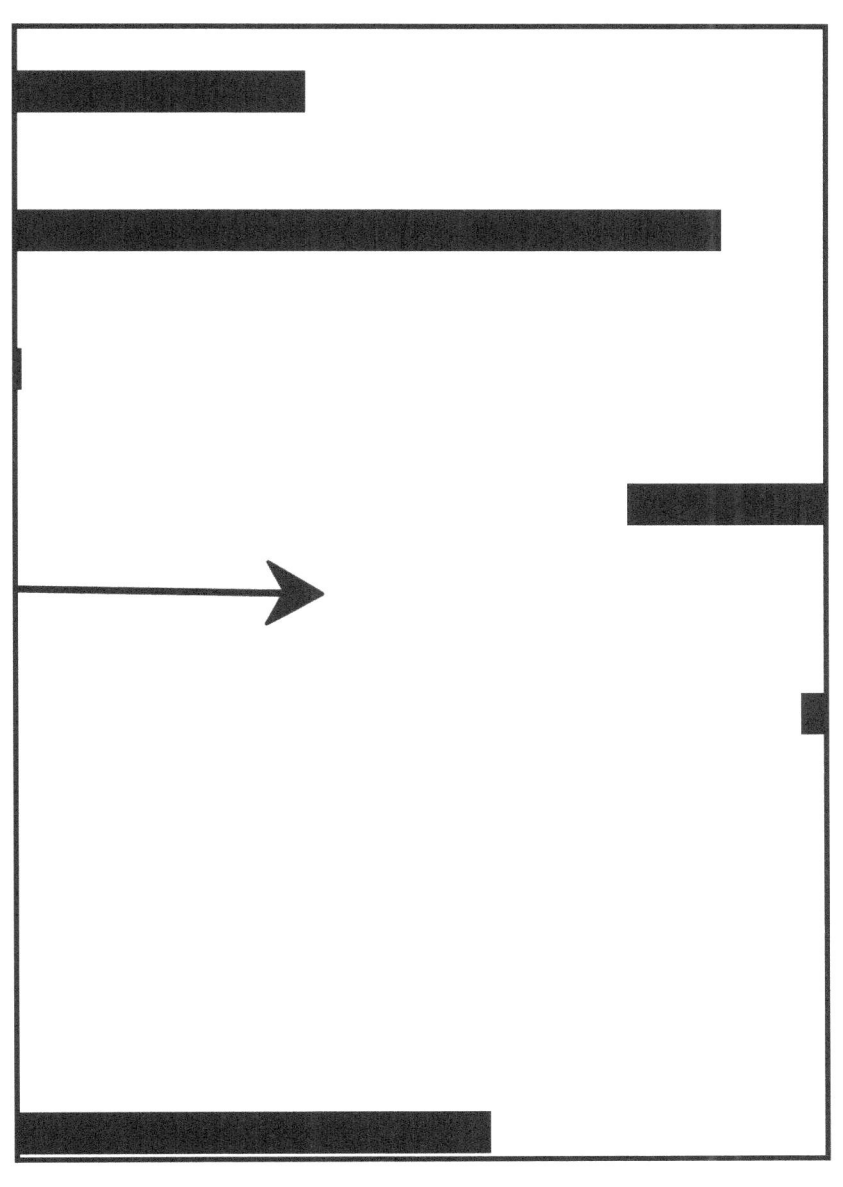

Chapter Six

Learning Self-Compassion

God loves you for you. Instead of beating yourself up, extend self-compassion as you identify the problem and find a solution. Be kinder to yourself—not only physically—but within the thoughts you have surrounding your shortcomings. Know it is okay to reschedule where needed so you can have the time you need to be successful as you move forward with hope.

Choose Your Target: Keep things simple and reduce the chance for overthrow. This section helps you pick one target to focus on each chapter and knock down the barriers in your way.

What areas do you tend to beat yourself up about? *Make a list.*

_____

_____

_____

_____

_____

_____

_____

_____

_____

_____

_____

_____

_____

_____

_____

_____

_____

_____

_____

_____

_____

_____

_____

_____

_____

_____

_____

Circle the areas where you are most likely to beat yourself up almost daily. Pick five to consider.

_____

_____

_____

_____

_____

From the five above, put a heart next to the three areas you are hardest on yourself. Write them here.

1 _____

2 _____

3 _____

Looking at the three hearts, which one area can you begin making changes to showcase self-compassion?

_____

_____

_____

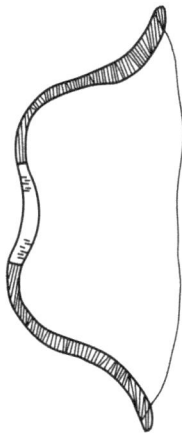

Raise Your Bow: You cannot shoot an arrow without a bow. This section helps you keep a list of tools and resources needed to help you hit your target.

Keep in mind the one area you are hardest on yourself and want to change now. What tools or resources do you need to begin showing self-compassion in this specific area?

_____

_____

_____

_____

_____

_____

_____

_____

_____

_____

_____

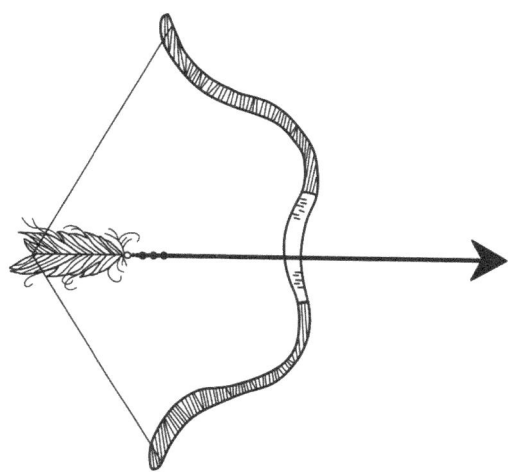

The Draw: Like pulling the bowstring back, this section takes a closer look at each chapter's highlights and the deeper lessons they hold.

If I want to serve others more, I have to first help myself create an environment I can sustain long term.

What parts of your environment are working for you?

_____

_____

_____

_____

What changes do you need to make within your environment to help you sustain it long term?

_____

_____

_____

_____

How do these changes help you serve others more?

_____

_____

_____

_____

_____

Having clearly defined boundaries helps reduce the amount of stress incurred when you uphold them.

What boundaries do you currently have in place within your career, business, ministry, or even personal life?

_____

_____

_____

_____

_____

What boundaries do you wish you had in place?

_____

_____

_____

_____

_____

What one boundary can you implement now?

_____

_____

_____

_____

_____

When things don't go as planned, practice responding in kindness and love instead of reacting harshly from a place of stress.

How do you typically respond when things don't go as planned?

_____

_____

_____

_____

_____

_____

_____

_____

How do you wish you could better respond during high stress situations?

_____

_____

_____

_____

_____

_____

_____

What is one thing you can do that will help redirect your response from negative to positive during moments of stress?

_____

_____

_____

_____

_____

Centered Aim: If you want to hit the bullseye, center your aim. This section recaps the chapter's scripture and prayer.

> *"After all, no one ever hated their own body, but they feed and care for their body, just as Christ does the church."*
>
> Ephesians 5:29

> *"The LORD appeared to us in the past, saying: 'I have loved you with an everlasting love; I have drawn you with unfailing kindness.'"*
>
> Jeremiah 31:3

Prayer:

> *Father, I am so sorry that I have neglected myself in a way that contributes to my overall stress. Help me let go of negative self-talk and actions while learning to pick up affirming conversation and prioritizing my needs. Please forgive me for allowing my negative mood to spill over into my daily interactions. Amen.*

Follow Through: To prevent premature dropping of the bow arm, a strong archer maintains their form after release. This section is a space for you to plan and track your steps.

What can you do now to start putting yourself first and showing more self-compassion?

_____
_____
_____
_____
_____
_____
_____
_____
_____
_____
_____
_____
_____

What steps do you need to take to start now?

_____

_____

_____

_____

_____

_____

_____

_____

_____

_____

_____

_____

_____

_____

_____

_____

_____

_____

_____

_____

_____

What is the deadline to complete this?

_____

_____

_____

After completing this section, add the steps needed as tasks in your to-do list. Set important dates and reminders to stay on target for your deadline date.

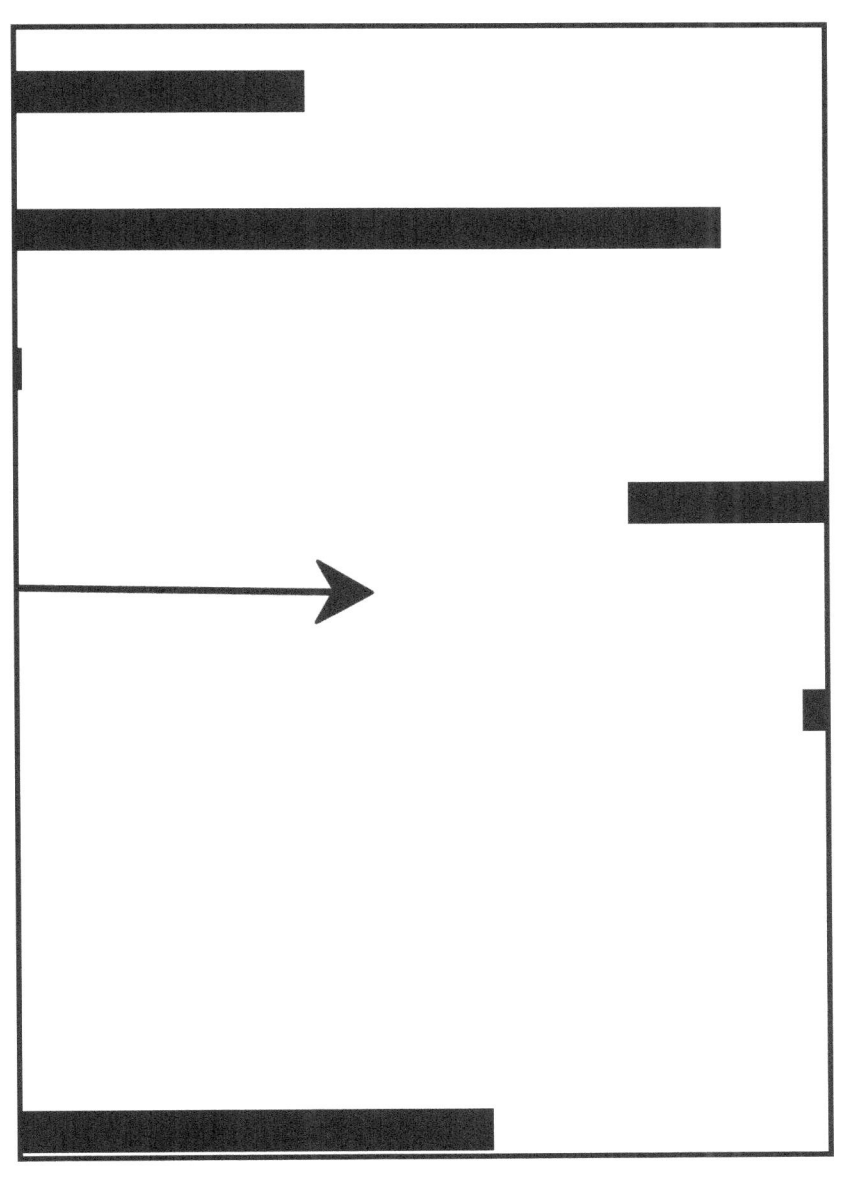

Chapter Seven

Mindset and Presence

We are all given the same twenty-four hours in a day. How we choose to spend them is entirely up to us. How much of the time spent is in alignment with God's will for your life? By focusing on strategic planning with a positive mindset, you can bring balance back to your schedule and find time to spend it in conversation with God daily as you move forward with hope.

Choose Your Target: Keep things simple and reduce the chance for overthrow. This section helps you pick one target to focus on each chapter and knock down the barriers in your way.

Consider the ways you plan your daily schedule. Make a list of every single step you take in your planning habits. Include the tools you use for each step. For example: Google Calendar for daily reminders, paper planner for weekly planning, or digital planner for access on multiple devices.

Tool	Task

As you look at your steps and tools, what feeling surfaces? Is it overwhelming, or do you feel peace?

_____

_____

_____

_____

Are there any steps or tools you can simplify? Put a star next to the ones that could be simplified. Write down three to focus on here.

1 _____

2 _____

3 _____

Pick one step or tool from the three above and begin working on a way to simplify this.

_____

_____

_____

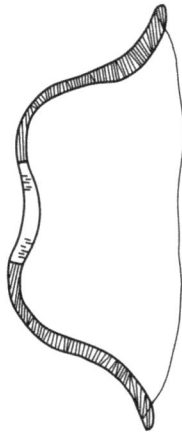

Raise Your Bow: You cannot shoot an arrow without a bow. This section helps you keep a list of tools and resources needed to help you hit your target.

Keep in mind the one step or tool you want to simplify. What tools or resources do you need to take away, and what ones do you need to implement?

_____

_____

_____

_____

_____

_____

_____

_____

_____

_____

_____

_____

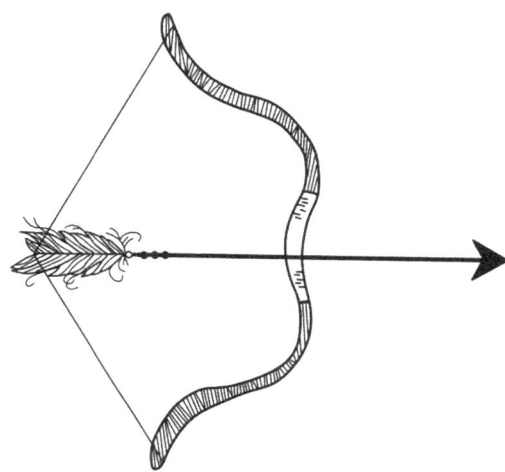

The Draw: Like pulling the bowstring back, this section takes a closer look at each chapter's highlights and the deeper lessons they hold.

Once you regain your balance, alignment will easily follow, as both work together in perfect harmony to help you move forward and fulfill your purpose.

What areas in your life feel out of balance?

_____

_____

_____

_____

In what ways can you regain balance in these areas?

_____

_____

_____

_____

What will align once you regain your balance?

_____

_____

_____

_____

_____

Focusing on the true, noble, right, pure, lovely, and admirable things keeps us on target.

What negative things are you allowing your mind to focus on?

_____

_____

_____

_____

_____

What can you do to change this negative thinking into more positive thinking?

_____

_____

_____

_____

_____

What scripture can help you remember to maintain a positive mindset?

_____

_____

_____

_____

_____

I trust that God has good plans for me today, and I will walk in His purpose with joy.

When things throw your schedule off, how do you react?

_____
_____
_____
_____
_____
_____
_____

What would help you better respond to a shift in schedule in a positive way?

_____
_____
_____
_____
_____

In what ways can you discover what God's plans for you are during a schedule shift beyond your control?

_____
_____
_____
_____
_____
_____
_____

Centered Aim: If you want to hit the bullseye, center your aim. This section recaps the chapter's scripture and prayer.

"Finally, brothers and sisters, whatever is true, whatever is noble, whatever is right, whatever is pure, whatever is lovely, whatever is admirable—if anything is excellent or praiseworthy—think about such things."

Philippians 4:8

"There is a time for everything, and a season for every activity under the heavens."

Ecclesiastes 3:1

Prayer:

Father, I am so sorry that I have maintained an unbalanced schedule and neglected time spent with you. Help me let go of becoming negative when there are delays and shifts in my schedule, causing the need for a pivot that may leave me feeling more stressed. Please forgive me for allowing my time to be spent on things that do not matter. I promise to rectify this by scheduling more time on the things that are pleasing to you. Amen.

Follow Through: To prevent premature dropping of the bow arm, a strong archer maintains their form after release. This section is a space for you to plan and track your steps.

It is up to us to ensure we are not only present daily, but that we approach each day with a positive mindset. What change can you make right now to help simplify your schedule?

_____
_____
_____
_____
_____
_____
_____
_____
_____
_____
_____
_____

What steps do you need to take to start now?

_____

_____

_____

_____

_____

_____

_____

_____

_____

_____

_____

_____

_____

_____

_____

_____

_____

_____

_____

_____

_____

_____

What is the deadline to complete this?

_____

_____

_____

After completing this section, add the steps needed as tasks in your to-do list. Set important dates and reminders to stay on target for your deadline date.

94 | Called to Serve

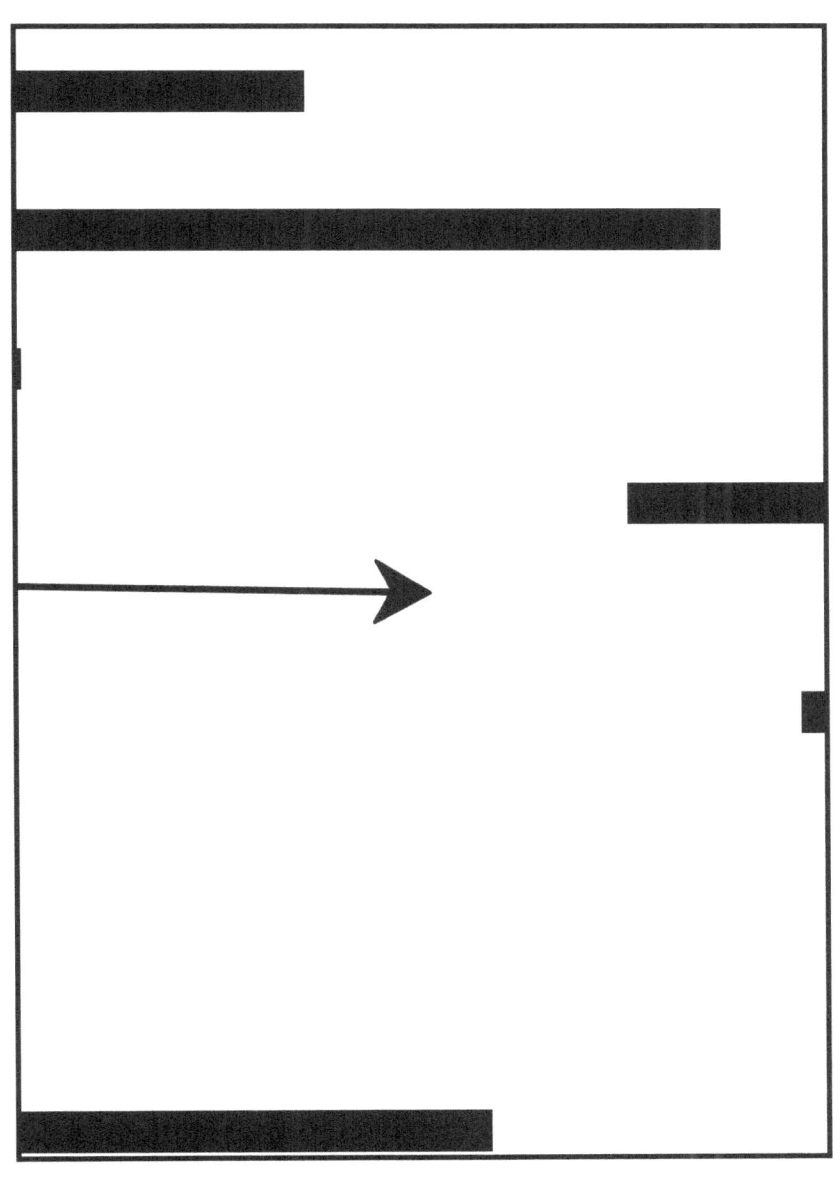

Chapter Eight

Don't Fear Change

change has the power to create resiliency in uncertainty. Using your positive mindset when faced with a challenge will help you get through this trial and get back on top again. How can you take everything you've learned and put it towards the transformation of your situation? Having the bravery to move forward with hope is an excellent place to start.

Choose Your Target: Keep things simple and reduce the chance for overthrow. This section helps you pick one target to focus on each chapter and knock down the barriers in your way.

What changes in your life have happened that have severely shifted your direction?

_____

_____

_____

_____

_____

_____

_____

_____

_____

_____

_____

_____

_____

_____

_____

_____

_____

_____

_____

_____

_____

_____

_____

_____

_____

_____

_____

Looking back at the changes in your life, did you learn any valuable lessons in any of them? If so, put a star next to all the ones that left an impact. Write down five to look at closer.

_____

_____

_____

_____

_____

From this list of five, what three changes in your life that would make a great teachable moment for someone else?

1 _____

2 _____

3 _____

Of the three you chose, which one change could you turn into a teachable lesson right now?

_____

_____

_____

Check In: We've reached halfway, how do you feel right now with your progress?

_____

_____

_____

_____

_____

_____

_____

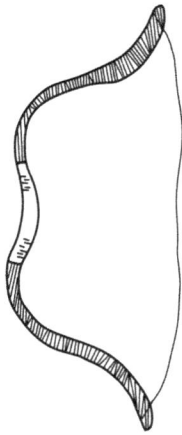

Raise Your Bow: You cannot shoot an arrow without a bow. This section helps you keep a list of tools and resources needed to help you hit your target.

Keep in mind the one change you can turn into a teachable moment now. What tools or resources do you need to begin outlining the teachable moment? Include any tools or resources needed to take this outline and put it into existence, whether it's a course, a book, or a presentation.

_____

_____

_____

_____

_____

_____

_____

_____

_____

_____

_____

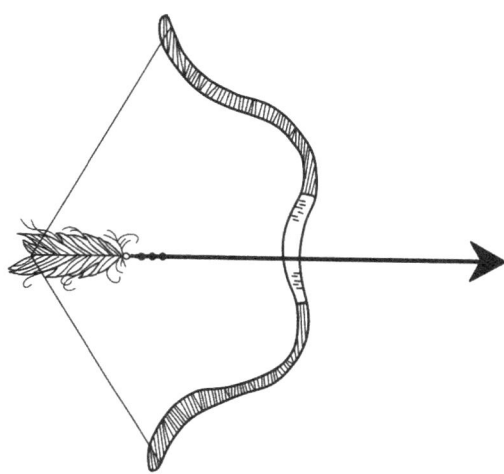

The Draw: Like pulling the bowstring back, this section takes a closer look at each chapter's highlights and the deeper lessons they hold.

The more I step out in faith, the more God shows me where His hand is my safety net.

Where can you start stepping out in faith more?

_____

_____

_____

_____

What control of your situation can you let go of to allow God to present His hand in the situation?

_____

_____

_____

_____

_____

What does it feel like to step out blindly in faith?

_____

_____

_____

_____

Be brave, friend.

Change has the power to create resiliency in uncertainty.

When faced with a forced change, how can you approach this new change with an open mind to see it as a new opportunity presented by God?

_____

_____

_____

_____

If you are struggling with feeling uncertain, what can you do to fully trust God more?

_____

_____

_____

_____

How can you challenge yourself to face change differently?

_____

_____

_____

_____

_____

Centered Aim: If you want to hit the bullseye, center your aim. This section recaps the chapter's scripture and prayer.

> *"'For I know the plans I have for you,' declares the LORD, 'plans to prosper you and not harm you, plans to give you hope and a future.'"*
> Jeremiah 29:11

> *"I the LORD do not change. So you, the descendants of Jacob, are not destroyed."*
> Malachi 3:6

Prayer:

> *Father, I am so sorry I didn't consider this change as your way of gently guiding me back on track. Help me let go of being frozen in place as stress and anxiety have taken over, and allow me to move forward again. Please forgive me for not trusting Your loving direction in my life. Amen.*

Follow Through: To prevent premature dropping of the bow arm, a strong archer maintains their form after release. This section is a space for you to plan and track your steps.

What do you need to do right now to begin teaching your teachable moment?

_____

_____

_____

_____

_____

_____

_____

_____

_____

_____

_____

_____

_____

_____

What steps do you need to take to start now?

_____

_____

_____

_____

_____

_____

_____

_____

_____

_____

_____

_____

_____

_____

_____

_____

_____

_____

_____

_____

What is the deadline to complete this?

_____

_____

_____

After completing this section, add the steps needed as tasks in your to-do list. Set important dates and reminders to stay on target for your deadline date.

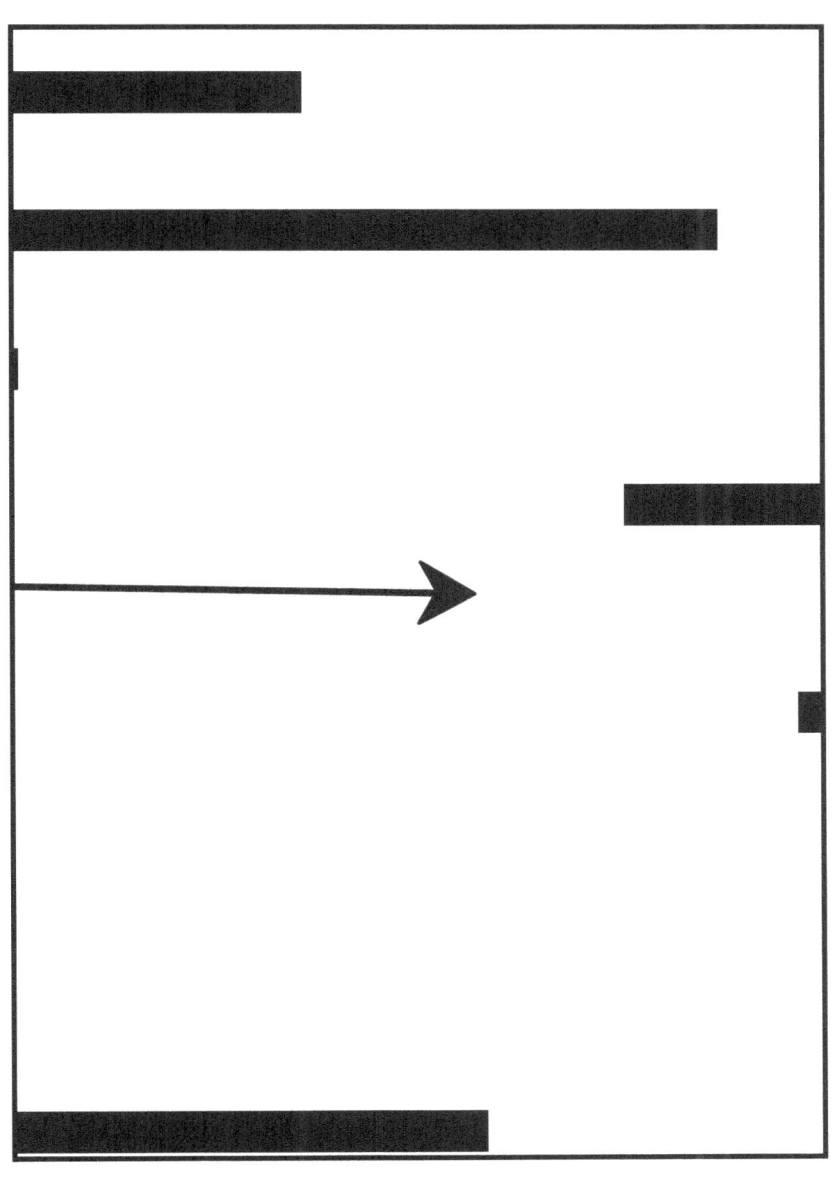

Chapter Nine

Surrender and Trust

If what you have been doing all along isn't working any longer, perhaps it's time to surrender and trust God. How would it feel to welcome in a sense of peace where once was stress? By surrendering and trusting, you can reduce the overwhelm you are causing in your life as you live in a way that prioritizes leaning into God's guidance instead of running blindly. I don't know about you, but just the thought of that makes me feel so grateful for all God does for me.

Choose Your Target: Keep things simple and reduce the chance for overthrow. This section helps you pick one target to focus on each chapter and knock down the barriers in your way.

In what areas are you trying to control the outcome right now? List them in different columns to cover faith, lifestyle, and business or career.

Faith	Lifestyle	Business/Career

In each column, circle six areas you wish you could surrender and trust God with right now.

From the areas circled, choose five to consider.

_____

_____

_____

_____

_____

From the five areas, choose three to consider surrendering now.

1 _____

2 _____

3 _____

From the three areas, choose one to begin surrendering now.

_____

_____

_____

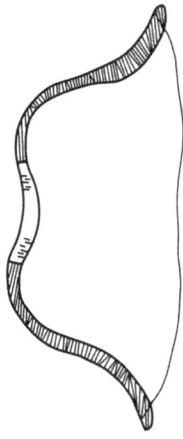

Raise Your Bow: You cannot shoot an arrow without a bow. This section helps you keep a list of tools and resources needed to help you hit your target.

Keep in mind the one area you need to surrender right now. What tools or resources do you need to make changes necessary to surrender your control and trust God's guidance?

_____

_____

_____

_____

_____

_____

_____

_____

_____

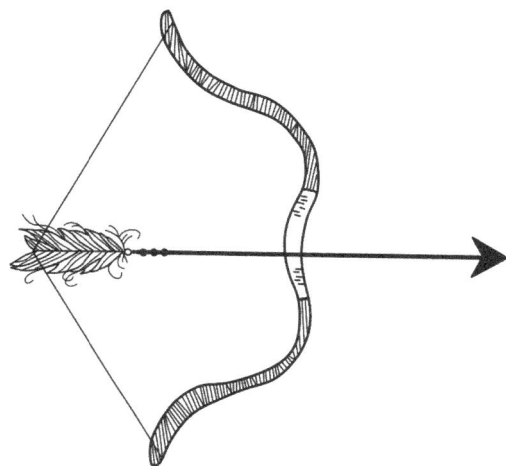

The Draw: Like pulling the bowstring back, this section takes a closer look at each chapter's highlights and the deeper lessons they hold.

I trust because of this alignment with God's purpose and will for my life, the seeds I have been planting will grow, allowing me to harvest them when the time is right.

What seeds have you been planting in the lives of others?

_____

_____

_____

_____

How do you feel when you cannot harvest the seeds you tried planting?

_____

_____

_____

_____

How can you surrender and trust that God will allow the harvesting when the time is right to the person He is wanting to harvest them?

_____

_____

_____

_____

Am I doing this for others or am I doing this for God?

Answer this question in the space provided. Be specific in what "this" is for you.

_____

_____

_____

_____

_____

_____

_____

_____

_____

Do you know what He is asking of you?

_____

_____

_____

_____

_____

_____

_____

Surrendering isn't a sign of weakness, but an admirable strength that can only exist within someone who stands bravely in their faith.

What strengths exist from you surrendering to God?

_____

_____

_____

_____

_____

_____

_____

How can you bravely stand in your faith?

_____

_____

_____

_____

_____

_____

_____

How would it feel to welcome in a sense of peace where once was stress?

_____

_____

_____

_____

_____

_____

_____

Centered Aim: If you want to hit the bullseye, center your aim. This section recaps the chapter's scripture and prayer.

> *"But blessed is the one who trusts in the LORD, whose confidence is in him. They will be like a tree planted by the water that sends out its roots by the stream. It does not fear when heat comes; its leaves are always green. It has no worries in a year of drought and never fails to bear fruit."*
>
> Jeremiah 17:7-8

> *"Commit to the LORD whatever you do, and he will establish your plans."*
>
> Proverbs 16:3

Prayer:

Father, I am so sorry that I kept running away from you as I stubbornly tried to do everything on my own. Help me let go of the need to control my destination and trust your loving guidance. Please forgive me for not asking for your help sooner. Amen.

Follow Through: To prevent premature dropping of the bow arm, a strong archer maintains their form after release. This section is a space for you to plan and track your steps.

We are no longer controlling our destiny; we are surrendering and trusting God to direct us. What do you need to do to begin surrendering and trusting God more?

_____

_____

_____

_____

_____

_____

_____

_____

_____

_____

_____

Surrender and Trust | 117

What steps do you need to take to start now?

_____

_____

_____

_____

_____

_____

_____

_____

_____

_____

_____

_____

_____

_____

_____

_____

_____

_____

_____

_____

_____

_____

What is the deadline to complete this?

_____

_____

_____

After completing this section, add the steps needed as tasks in your to-do list. Set important dates and reminders to stay on target for your deadline date.

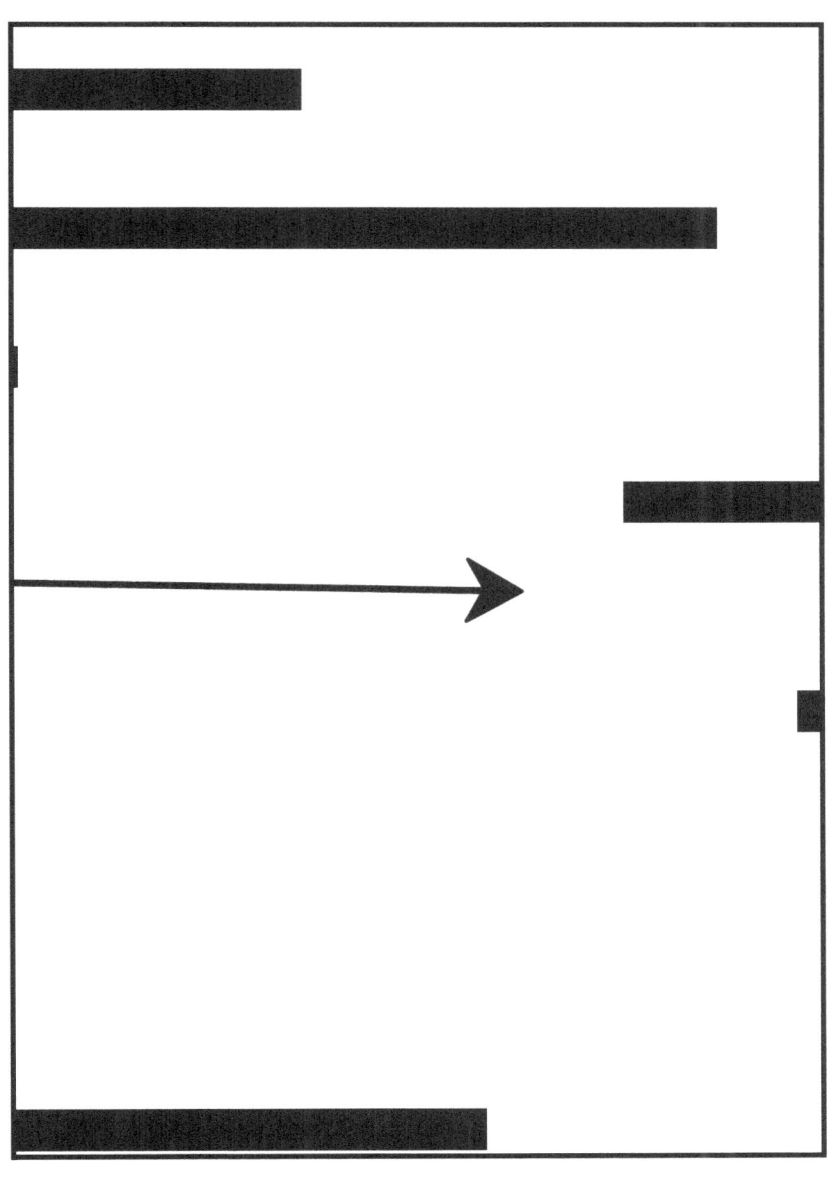

chapter Ten

A Spirit of Gratitude

Expressing gratitude for those who have supported you strengthens your bond with them as they feel seen, heard, and appreciated for the role they had in helping you. When was the last time you reciprocated that help to your friends during their time of need?

Choose Your Target: Keep things simple and reduce the chance for overthrow. This section helps you pick one target to focus on each chapter and knock down the barriers in your way.

Make a list of friends and loved ones you are grateful to have in your life. Include a short statement of why you are grateful for them.

_____

_____

_____

_____

_____

_____

_____

_____

_____

_____

_____

_____

_____

_____

_____

_____

_____

_____

_____

_____

_____

_____

_____

_____

_____

_____

_____

_____

_____

_____

As you read your list of names, put a heart next to the ones you know are going through a difficult time right now. Pick five that stand out the most to you.

_____

_____

_____

_____

_____

Considering the five, pick three names of the individuals who have helped you during a time of need.

1 _____

2 _____

3 _____

Pick one of the three names to give help back to them now in any way you can.

_____

_____

_____

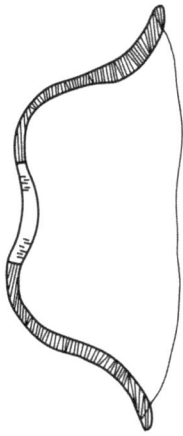

Raise Your Bow: You cannot shoot an arrow without a bow. This section helps you keep a list of tools and resources needed to help you hit your target.

Keep in mind the one friend you are going to help now. What tools or resources do you need to help them through their difficult time?

_____

_____

_____

_____

_____

_____

_____

_____

_____

_____

_____

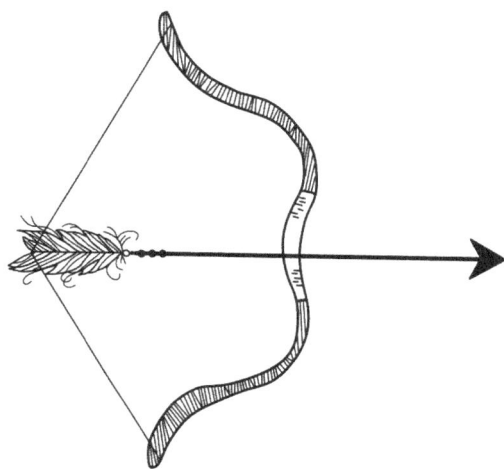

The Draw: Like pulling the bowstring back, this section takes a closer look at each chapter's highlights and the deeper lessons they hold.

By fostering a spirit of gratitude—even when we fail, we recondition ourselves to think vastly differently than we have in the past.

When you experience failure, how difficult is it for you to be grateful?

_____

_____

_____

_____

_____

What is something you can do to express gratitude when you fail?

_____

_____

_____

_____

A Spirit of Gratitude |

If you think back to a moment you felt you failed, can you see something now to be grateful for? What is it?

_____

_____

_____

_____

_____

Gratitude has flipped the script on me, taking me from seeing what I don't have and showing me what God has already done.

What areas has God brought you victory?

_____

_____

_____

_____

_____

What lessons did God teach you during moments you felt like a failure?

_____

_____

_____

_____

_____

How can you search for moments to be grateful for when you aren't feeling a spirit of gratitude?

_____

_____

_____

Centered Aim: If you want to hit the bullseye, center your aim. This section recaps the chapter's scripture and prayer.

> *"Give thanks in all circumstances; for this is God's will for you in Christ Jesus."*
>
> 1 Thessalonians 5:18

> *"I thank my God every time I remember you. In all my prayers for all of you, I always pray with joy because of your partnership in the gospel from the first day until now."*
>
> Philippians 1:3-5

Prayer:

> *Father, I am so sorry that I blindly focused on my trials and how they were affecting me instead of seeing all the goodness that surrounded me despite it all. Help me let go of the negative outlook I place on the trials I face. Please forgive me for not appreciating the friends you brought to me, and all they have done for me throughout the years. Amen.*

Follow Through: To prevent premature dropping of the bow arm, a strong archer maintains their form after release. This section is a space for you to plan and track your steps.

What do you need to do right now to begin reciprocating help for your friend?

_____

_____

_____

_____

_____

_____

_____

_____

_____

_____

_____

_____

_____

What steps do you need to take to start now?

_____

_____

_____

_____

_____

_____

_____

_____

_____

_____

_____

_____

_____

_____

_____

_____

_____

_____

_____

What is the deadline to complete this?

_____

_____

_____

After completing this section, add the steps needed as tasks in your to-do list.
Set important dates and reminders to stay on target for your deadline date.

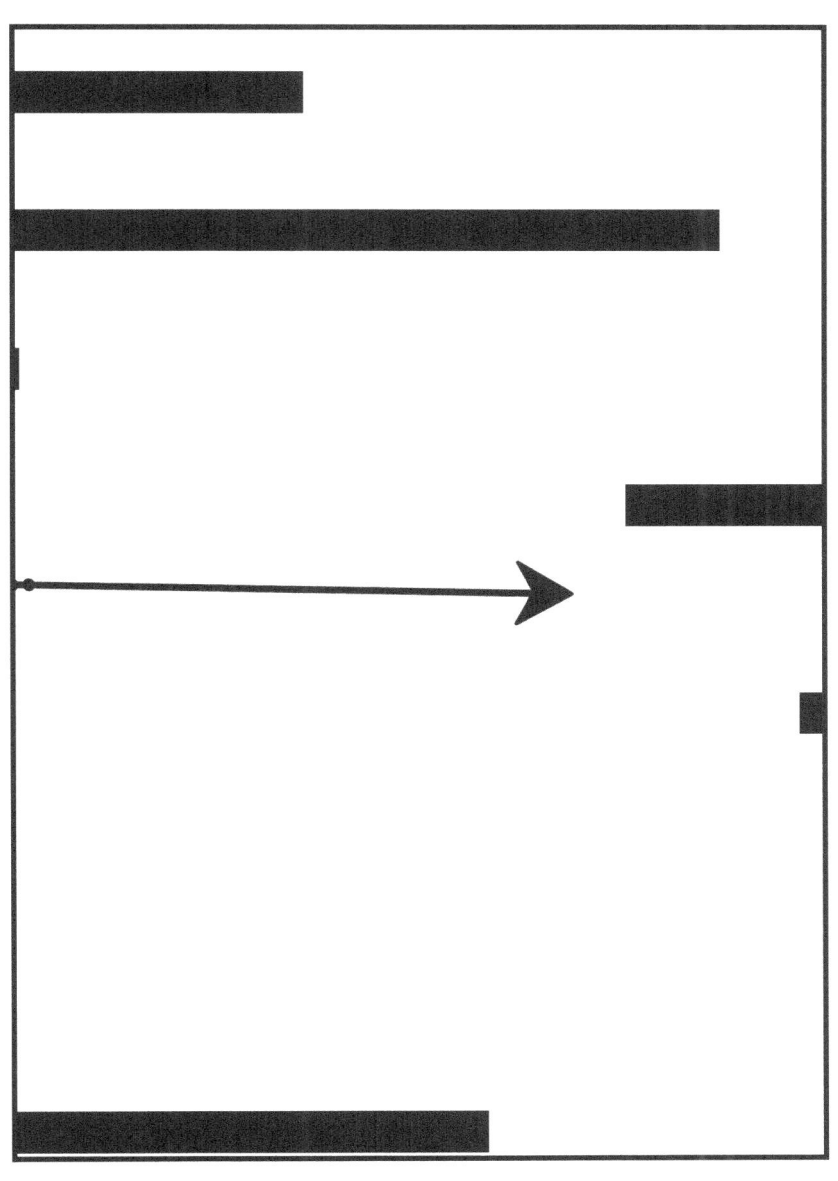

Chapter Eleven

Hopeful Future

Being the change this world needs means to lead in love. Say yes to the calling God is placing on your heart to be a servant leader. Focus on setting the example by letting others see God work in and through you without condemning them or their actions. By allowing yourself to love like Jesus, you become braver with belief more than ever.

Choose Your Target: Keep things simple and reduce the chance for overthrow. This section helps you pick one target to focus on each chapter and knock down the barriers in your way.

In what ways do you believe you can be the change this world needs? Make a list of everything that comes to mind.

_____

_____

_____

_____

_____

_____

_____

_____

_____

_____

_____

_____

_____

_____

_____

_____

_____

_____

_____

_____

_____

_____

_____

_____

_____

_____

_____

As you review your list, which areas do you feel God calling you to be a servant leader? Put a heart next to them. Pick five to consider closer.

_____

_____

_____

_____

_____

From your list of five, narrow it down to three that stand out to you the most.

1 _____

2 _____

3 _____

Which one area from your list of three can you focus on right now to explore as the foundation of what you will do next?

_____

_____

_____

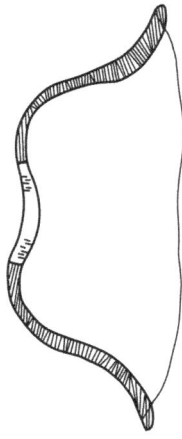

Raise Your Bow: You cannot shoot an arrow without a bow. This section helps you keep a list of tools and resources needed to help you hit your target.

Keep in mind the one area you focus on right now. What tools or resources do you need to begin building the foundation of an answer to your calling?

_____

_____

_____

_____

_____

_____

_____

_____

_____

_____

_____

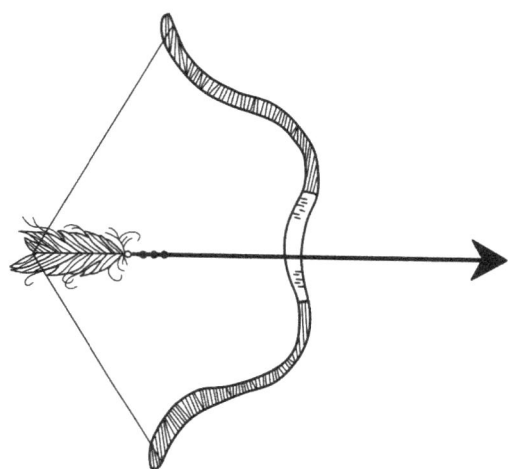

The Draw: Like pulling the bowstring back, this section takes a closer look at each chapter's pull quotes and the deeper lessons they hold.

If you are unwilling to change into the woman God is calling you to be, you cannot be the servant leader others need.

What areas do you feel you need to change to become who God is calling you to be?

_____

_____

_____

_____

How can you let go of the struggle within and step into the wholeness of who God created you to be?

_____

_____

_____

You can be respectful of others' beliefs while still honoring yours.

How can you begin putting this into practice now?

_____

_____

_____

_____

What does it mean to you to 'be respectful of others' beliefs'?

_____

_____

_____

_____

How can you honor your beliefs while still being respectful of others?

_____

_____

_____

_____

Knowing God is calling you to be a servant leader is less about an obvious revelation and more about a deep, persistent stirring within your spirit.

What has been a deep, persistent stirring within your spirit you've noticed?

_____

_____

_____

_____

_____

How can you explore this as a possible area to be a servant leader for God?

_____

_____

_____

_____

_____

Write out anything that comes to mind when you consider the possibility of saying yes to becoming a servant leader in this area.

_____

_____

_____

_____

_____

_____

_____

_____

_____

_____

_____

_____

_____

_____

_____

_____

_____

_____

Change begins with you.

Centered Aim: If you want to hit the bullseye, center your aim. This section recaps the chapter's scripture and prayer.

"My command is this: Love each other as I have loved you. Greater love has no one than this: to lay down one's life for one's friends."
John 15:12-13

"A new command I give you: Love one another. As I have loved you, so you must love one another."
John 13:34

"Above all, love each other deeply, because love covers a multitude of sins."
1 Peter 4:8

Prayer:
Father, I am so sorry I was quick to judge others who differ from me. Help me let go of the need to be right in my stance and open my heart up to learn about the differences in others. Please forgive me for not being an example of your love in and through me. Amen.

Follow Through: To prevent premature dropping of the bow arm, a strong archer maintains their form after release. This section is a space for you to plan and track your steps.

If this one area is the foundation of what you will use to build from, what is it that you will be building?

_____

_____

_____

_____

_____

_____

_____

_____

_____

_____

_____

_____

_____

_____

What steps do you need to take to start now?

_____

_____

_____

_____

_____

_____

_____

_____

_____

_____

_____

_____

_____

_____

_____

_____

_____

_____

_____

_____

What is the deadline to complete this?

_____

_____

_____

After completing this section, add the steps needed as tasks in your to-do list.
Set important dates and reminders to stay on target for your deadline date.

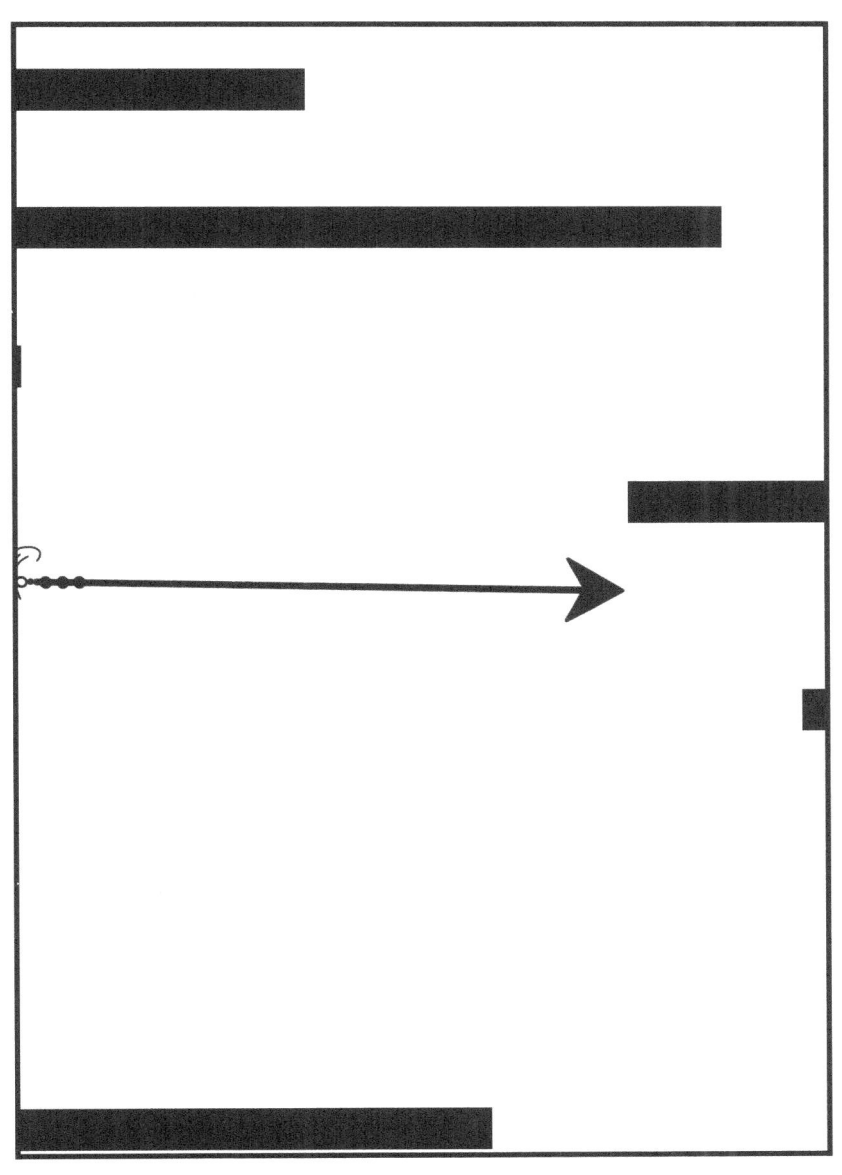

Chapter Twelve

Braver with Belief

Becoming braver with belief helps you become stronger and more resilient in your faith. You'll feel closer to God as your connection grows stronger and stronger. Once you've reached this point, you can then work towards serving others. Hearing and answering the call provides direction and clarity.

Choose Your Target: Keep things simple and reduce the chance for overthrow. This section helps you pick one target to focus on each chapter and knock down the barriers in your way.

What areas have you bent to please someone else by changing what you felt was the right thing to do to please them? List all that come to mind.

_____

_____

_____

_____

_____

_____

_____

_____

_____

_____

_____

_____

_____

_____

_____

_____

_____

_____

_____

_____

_____

_____

_____

_____

_____

_____

Of the areas you listed, circle the ones you wish you could do differently. Pick five of the circled areas that stick out to you most.

_____

_____

_____

_____

_____

Of the five, choose three that you are ready to focus on and revamp.

1 _____

2 _____

3 _____

Pick one of the three areas that you can revamp to align with your calling.

_____

_____

_____

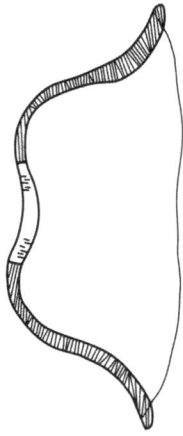

Raise Your Bow: You cannot shoot an arrow without a bow. This section helps you keep a list of tools and resources needed to help you hit your target.

Keep in mind the one area you want to revamp. What tools or resources do you need to begin developing it to be more in alignment with your calling?

_____

_____

_____

_____

_____

_____

_____

_____

_____

_____

_____

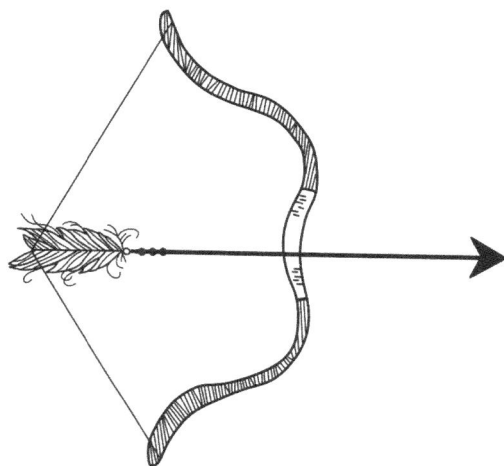

The Draw: Like pulling the bowstring back, this section takes a closer look at each chapter's pull quotes and the deeper lessons they hold.

When I think about what it means to be braver with belief, I see myself standing confidently as I share my love for the Lord.

What hesitations do you have around sharing your love for the Lord?

_____
_____
_____
_____
_____

What can help you gain confidence in this area?

_____
_____
_____
_____

To bravely stand up for what you believe in requires a level of self-discipline deeply rooted and driven only by God's love.

How can you remove the desire to please people as you make decisions that solely please God?

_____

_____

_____

_____

_____

How can you be firm, yet loving, in your "no" to others as you say yes to God?

_____

_____

_____

_____

_____

_____

Growth and readiness comes while walking in your calling, not in the preparation.

How can you let go of the desire to have the perfect plan in place before you step out and lead?

_____

_____

_____

_____

_____

_____

In what areas do you need to trust God more in the preparation of fulfilling your calling?

_____

_____

_____

_____

_____

_____

What is stopping you from starting now?

_____

_____

_____

_____

_____

_____

_____

_____

_____

_____

_____

_____

_____

_____

_____

_____

_____

Pray, friend. Simply pray.

Centered Aim: If you want to hit the bullseye, center your aim. This section recaps the chapter's scripture and prayer.

> *"When I am afraid, I put my trust in you. In God, whose word I praise—in God I trust and am not afraid. What can mere mortals do to me?"*
>
> Psalm 56:3-4

> *"For the Spirit God gave us does not make us timid, but gives us power, love and self-discipline."*
>
> 2 Timothy 1:7

Prayer:
> *Father, I am so sorry that I have put people above you as I bend to please them. Help me let go of being afraid to stand up for what I believe in while dimming the light you shine brightly within. Please forgive me for not relying on you like I should. Amen.*

Follow Through: To prevent premature dropping of the bow arm, a strong archer maintains their form after release. This section is a space for you to plan and track your steps.

What area will you choose to revamp: a product offering, a service, a ministry? How can you get it off the ground and running?

_____
_____
_____
_____
_____
_____
_____
_____
_____
_____
_____
_____
_____
_____

What steps do you need to take to start now?

_____

_____

_____

_____

_____

_____

_____

_____

_____

_____

_____

_____

_____

_____

_____

_____

_____

_____

_____

What is the deadline to complete this?

_____

_____

_____

After completing this section, add the steps needed as tasks in your to-do list. Set important dates and reminders to stay on target for your deadline date.

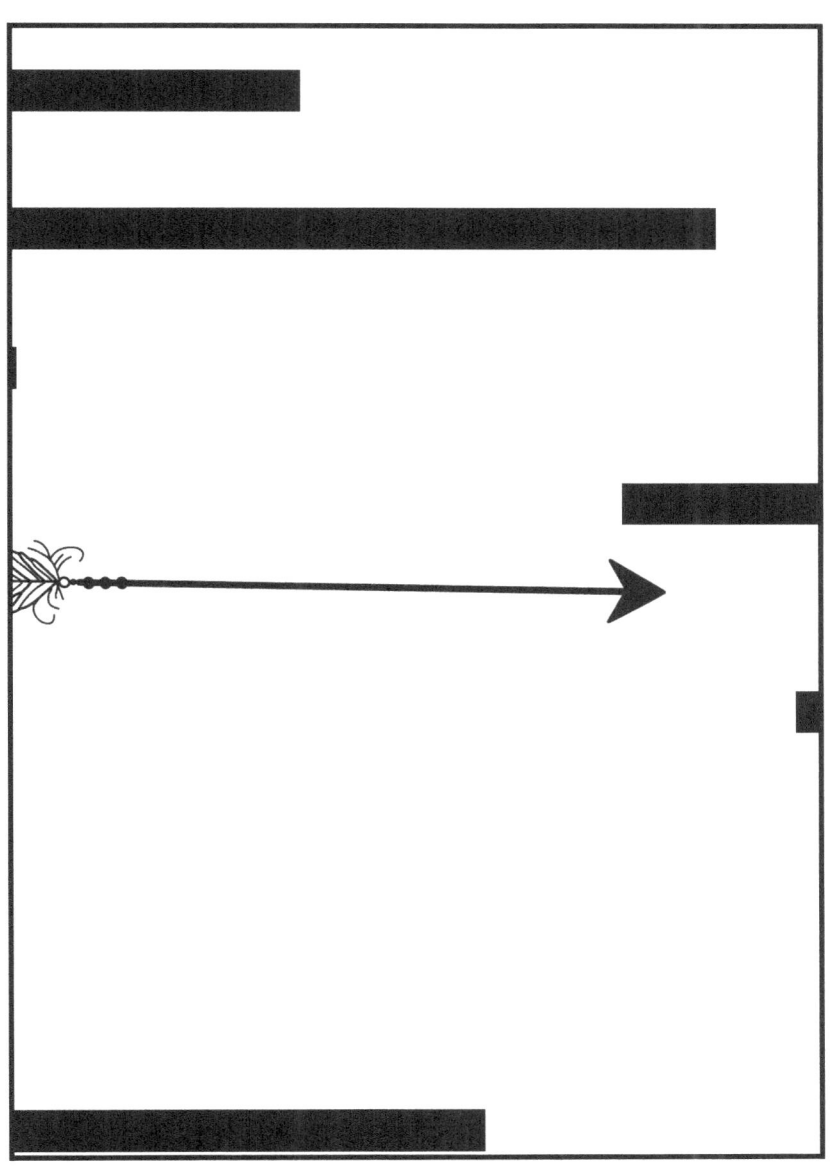

chapter Thirteen

A Sacred Dance

It is important to be receptive to His guidance. In allowing God the chance to work in and through you, your intentions and actions will change to be more in alignment with Him. Once you are ready, fully let go of all that you are clinging to as you say yes to what awaits you.

Choose Your Target: Keep things simple and reduce the chance for overthrow. This section helps you pick one target to focus on each chapter and knock down the barriers in your way.

Make a list of all the skills you have learned.

_____
_____
_____
_____
_____
_____
_____
_____
_____
_____
_____
_____
_____
_____

Make a list of all ways in which you feel you could serve others.

_____
_____
_____
_____
_____
_____
_____
_____
_____
_____
_____
_____
_____
_____

Pick your top five skills and pair them with a way to use them by serving others. You should have five different skills matched to five different ways to serve.

_____

_____

_____

_____

_____

From your list of five, pick the three that stand out to you most.

1 _____

2 _____

3 _____

Review your list of three and choose one skill and one way you could serve others using that skill right now. Write that here.

_____

_____

_____

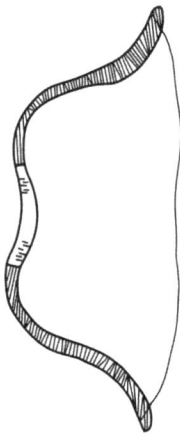

Raise Your Bow: You cannot shoot an arrow without a bow. This section helps you keep a list of tools and resources needed to help you hit your target.

Keep in mind the way you can serve others using the skill you chose. What tools or resources do you need to begin serving people now?

_____

_____

_____

_____

_____

_____

_____

_____

_____

_____

_____

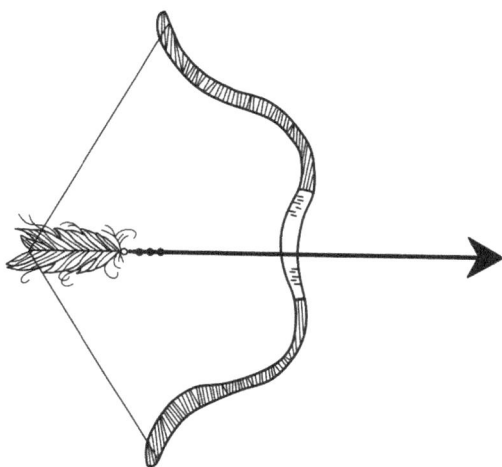

The Draw: Like pulling the bowstring back, this section takes a closer look at each chapter's pull quotes and the deeper lessons they hold.

No longer burdened by perfectionism, we find ourselves more purposefully following God's guidance.

By letting go of perfectionism, in what ways have you given yourself the chance to follow God's guidance?

_____

_____

_____

Where is God guiding you right now?

_____

_____

_____

_____

_____

Allowing my schedule to dictate my relationship with God, I found, was a disservice to both of us.

How can you maintain a schedule that allows God the chance to lead first?

_____

_____

_____

_____

_____

_____

_____

What old habits have you fallen into that have changed your schedule?

_____

_____

_____

_____

_____

_____

_____

What can you do going forward to ensure you do not fall back into these old habits?

_____

_____

_____

_____

_____

_____

_____

Centered Aim: If you want to hit the bullseye, center your aim. This section recaps the chapter's scripture and prayer.

"You turned my wailing into dancing; you removed my sackcloth and clothed me with joy, that my heart may sing your praises and not be silent. LORD my God, I will praise you forever."
Psalm 30:11-12

"Then I heard the voice of the LORD saying, 'Whom shall I send? And who will go for us?' And I said, 'Here am I. Send me!'"
Isaiah 6:8

Prayer:
Father, I am so sorry for clinging too tightly to my life. Help me let go fully as I trust more in you. Please forgive me for continually telling you I wasn't ready when you kept showing me I was. Amen.

Follow Through: To prevent premature dropping of the bow arm, a strong archer maintains their form after release. This section is a space for you to plan and track your steps.

What can you do right now to begin serving others using the skill and area you chose?

_____

_____

_____

_____

_____

_____

_____

_____

_____

_____

_____

_____

_____

What steps do you need to take to start now?

_____
_____
_____
_____
_____
_____
_____
_____
_____
_____
_____
_____
_____
_____
_____
_____ .
_____
_____
_____
_____
_____
_____

What is the deadline to complete this?

_____
_____
_____

*After completing this section, add the steps needed as tasks in your to-do list.
Set important dates and reminders to stay on target for your deadline date.*

A Sacred Dance | 165

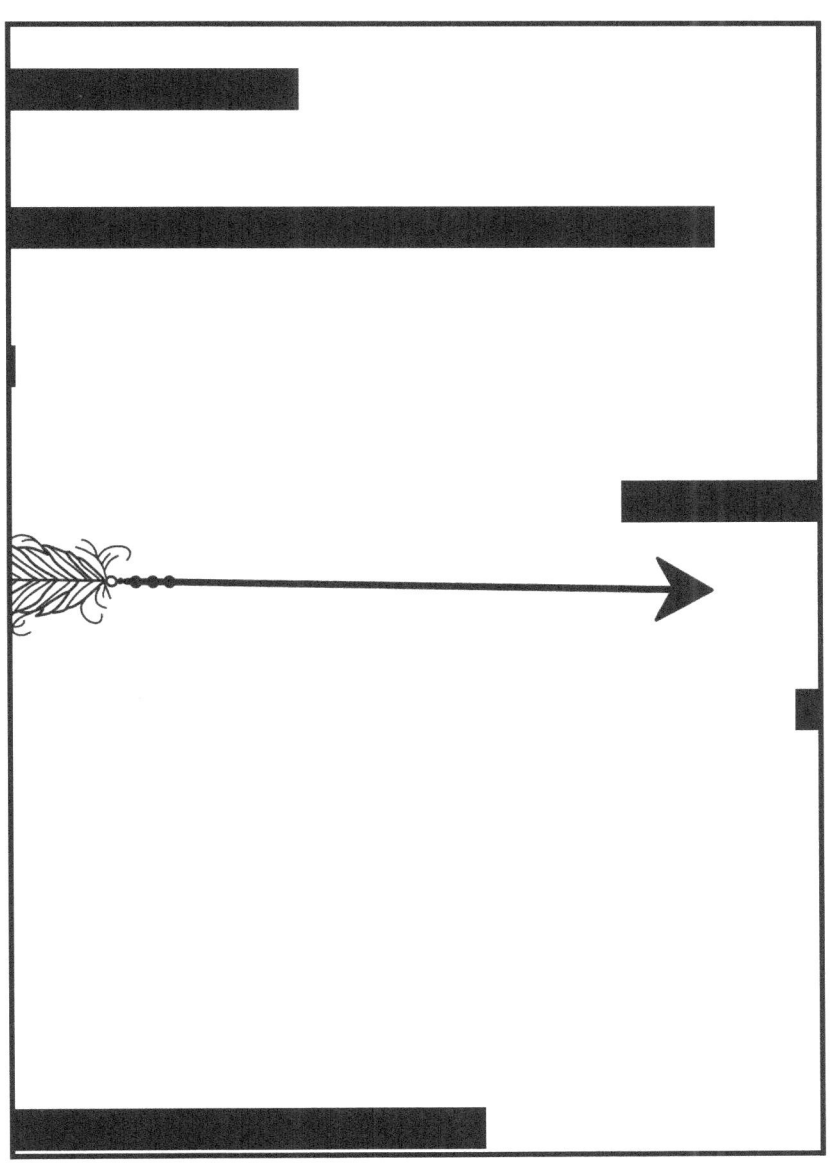

Chapter Fourteen

New Beginnings

Together, we are finally letting go of fear as we fill its place with excitement for what is yet to come. You have worked so hard to get to this point in your life. Slow down a bit to enjoy every moment along the way. Be brave in your change as you step out into this new beginning with a humble heart.

Choose Your Target: Keep things simple and reduce the chance for overthrow. This section helps you pick one target to focus on each chapter and knock down the barriers in your way.

Let's take your "yes" to servant leadership and define it in the tangible actions you will take to fulfill your calling.

Explore which area best fits your calling. Brainstorm topics and ideas under each of the categories provided that show a clear direction to take. *Come up with as many as you can, you may need a separate piece of paper.*

Launch or Relaunch a Business
Topics   Ideas

Write a Book
Topics   Ideas

Start a Ministry
Topics   Ideas

Reading back through your topics and ideas, put a star next to five ideas in each category and a heart next to five topics in each category that stands out to you as a strong possibility.

Narrow down your fifteen choices by choosing five topics and five ideas to consider paired together.

Topics	Ideas

Pick three that stand out to you from your list of five.

1 _____

2 _____

3 _____

The topic you choose will be paired with the idea to put into action. Spend some time in prayer over the next couple of days for the choices you have made. Ask God to direct you to the one He would like for you to choose right now.

Which one do you feel God is guiding you to do right now?

_____

_____

_____

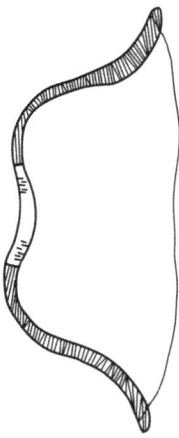

Raise Your Bow: You cannot shoot an arrow without a bow. This section helps you keep a list of tools and resources needed to help you hit your target.

Keep in mind the direction you were given. Whether it was to launch a business, write a book, or start a ministry, consider what you need to get started. What tools or resources do you need to put this idea into action?

_____
_____
_____
_____
_____
_____
_____
_____
_____
_____
_____
_____

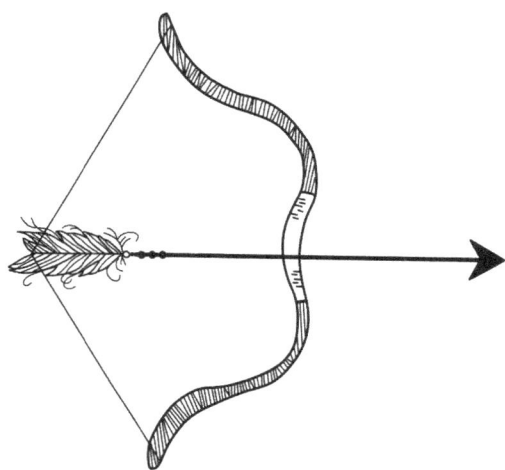

The Draw: Like pulling the bowstring back, this section takes a closer look at each chapter's pull quotes and the deeper lessons they hold.

The more you depend on God, the more clarity you have.

What can you do to show God that you are more dependent on His guidance now?

_____

_____

_____

_____

_____

How does it make you feel to trust that by depending more on God, He will help you gain clarity?

_____

_____

_____

_____

This new beginning you face is the start of a revival.

What kind of revival are you hoping to start right now?

_____

_____

_____

_____

_____

_____

_____

_____

_____

What do you hope others will feel as you lead them?

_____

_____

_____

_____

_____

_____

_____

_____

Are you ready to lead a new revival?

_____

_____

_____

_____

Centered Aim: If you want to hit the bullseye, center your aim. This section recaps the chapter's scripture and prayer.

> *"Therefore, if anyone is in Christ, the new creation has come: The old has gone, the new is here!"*
> 2 Corinthians 5:17

> *"He who was seated on the throne said, 'I am making everything new!' Then he said, 'Write this down, for these words are trustworthy and true.'"*
> Revelation 21:5

Prayer:
> *Father, I am so sorry for not inviting you to sit with me every time I work towards creating a future in serving you. Help me let go of waiting on direction and start inviting you to open my heart to see the signs you've lovingly placed around me. Please forgive me for thinking I could do all of this on my own. I need you now more than ever before. Amen.*

Follow Through: To prevent premature dropping of the bow arm, a strong archer maintains their form after release. This section is a space for you to plan and track your steps.

It's time for a new beginning. What do you need to do to begin working towards fulfilling the direction you've received?

_____

_____

_____

_____

_____

_____

_____

_____

_____

_____

_____

_____

_____

_____

What steps do you need to take to start now?

_____

_____

_____

_____

_____

_____

_____

_____

_____

_____

_____

_____

_____

_____

_____

_____

_____

_____

_____

_____

What is the deadline to complete this?

_____

_____

_____

After completing this section, add the steps needed as tasks in your to-do list. Set important dates and reminders to stay on target for your deadline date.

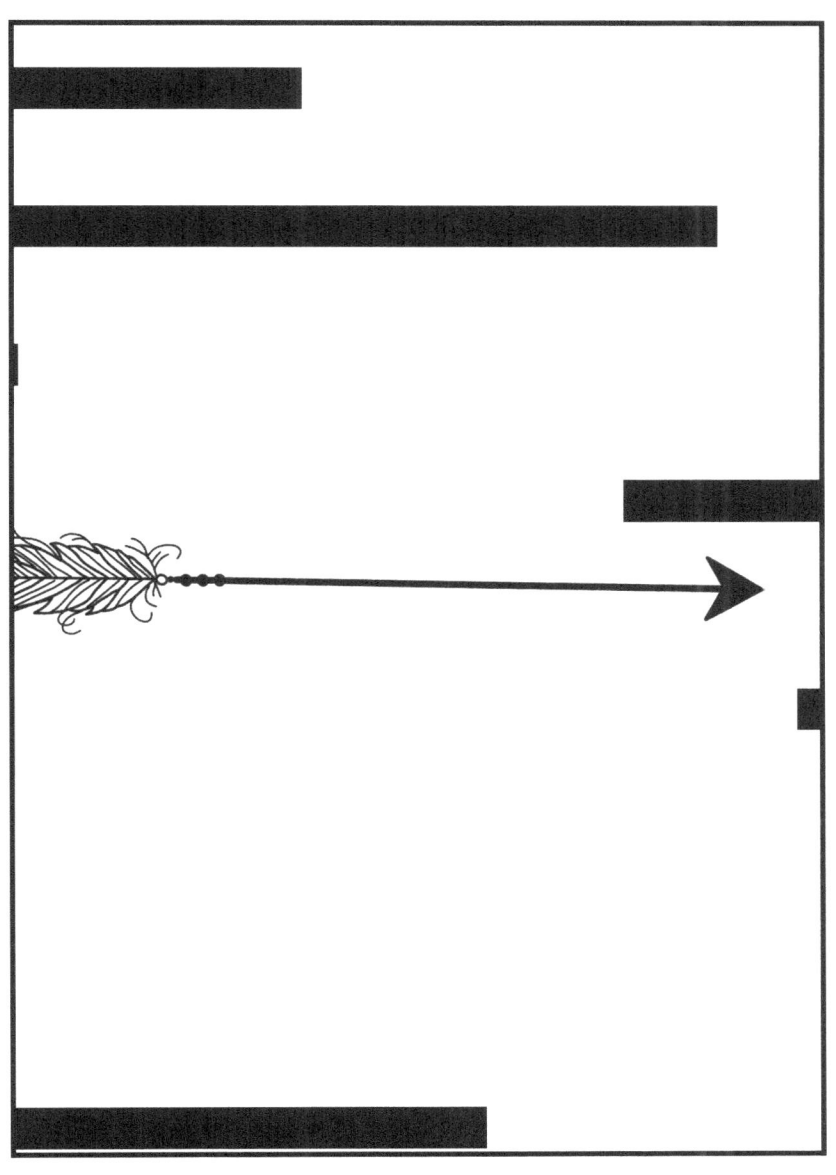

Chapter Fifteen

A Humble Heart

A humble heart recognizes the gifts God has given you; blessings from Him and not solely the result of your personal effort. Give thanks for the gifts He's given you to share with others. Don't hide your gifts by not using them in a way that honors God.

Choose Your Target: Keep things simple and reduce the chance for overthrow. This section helps you pick one target to focus on each chapter and knock down the barriers in your way.

Make a list of gifts God has given you that can be used as you serve others. Because we've already identified your skills earlier, we want to focus on the gifts found within your personality. Are you nurturing, determined, thoughtful, encouraging, or resourceful? Write down everything that comes to mind.

_____

_____

_____

_____

_____

_____

_____

_____

_____

_____

_____

_____

_____

_____

_____

_____

_____

_____

_____

_____

_____

_____

_____

_____

_____

_____

Of all the gifts you have written, put a heart next to ten that stand out to you the most as the top ten things you want to incorporate into your calling.

From your ten gifts with a heart next to them, pick five to focus on.

_____

_____

_____

_____

_____

Considering your five, pick your three strongest gifts.

1 _____

2 _____

3 _____

From your three gifts, choose one you can implement right now.

_____

_____

_____

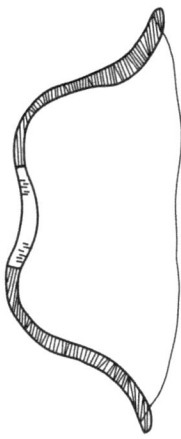

Raise Your Bow: You cannot shoot an arrow without a bow. This section helps you keep a list of tools and resources needed to help you hit your target.

Keep in mind the one gift you want to incorporate into your calling. What tools or resources do you need to create a service or offering around this gift?

_____

_____

_____

_____

_____

_____

_____

_____

_____

_____

_____

_____

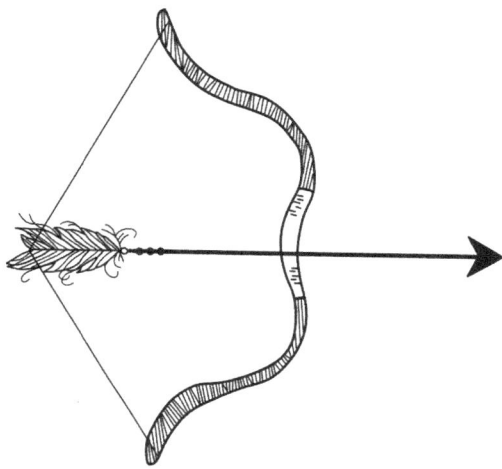

The Draw: Like pulling the bowstring back, this section takes a closer look at each chapter's highlights and the deeper lessons they hold.

When we agree to serve God, we must go through a refining of our heart and spirit to prepare us for what comes next.

In what areas have you been too prideful?

_____
_____
_____
_____
_____

How can you be more humble in these areas?

_____
_____
_____
_____
_____

As you become a servant leader, may you move forward with a humble heart, celebrating those whose lives you are changing for the glory of the Lord.

Ask God to prepare your heart to lead those He brings to you. How can you ensure you are ready to serve all He brings your way?

_____

_____

_____

_____

_____

How can you celebrate the lives of those brought to you by God?

_____

_____

_____

_____

_____

Healing is holy work that requires patience, trust, and surrender.

How can you maintain a spirit of patience, trust, and surrender as you serve?

_____

_____

_____

_____

_____

_____

Centered Aim: If you want to hit the bullseye, center your aim. This section recaps the chapter's scripture and prayer.

"Do nothing out of selfish ambition or vain conceit. Rather, in humility value others above yourselves."

Philippians 2:3

"Humble yourselves, therefore, under God's mighty hand, that he may lift you up in due time."

1 Peter 5:6

Prayer:

Father, I am so sorry for not always giving you the glory as I sought recognition. Help me let go of the need to always be the one talking and start practicing active listening. Please forgive me for not using my gifts to their fullest potential. I desire to always serve with a humble heart. Amen.

Follow Through: To prevent premature dropping of the bow arm, a strong archer maintains their form after release. This section is a space for you to plan and track your steps.

How can you build your offering,service, or ministry around your gift you chose to focus on now?

_____
_____
_____
_____
_____
_____
_____
_____
_____
_____
_____
_____
_____
_____

What steps do you need to take to start now?

_____
_____
_____
_____
_____
_____
_____
_____
_____
_____
_____
_____
_____
_____
_____
_____
_____
_____
_____
_____

What is the deadline to complete this?

_____
_____
_____

After completing this section, add the steps needed as tasks in your to-do list. Set important dates and reminders to stay on target for your deadline date.

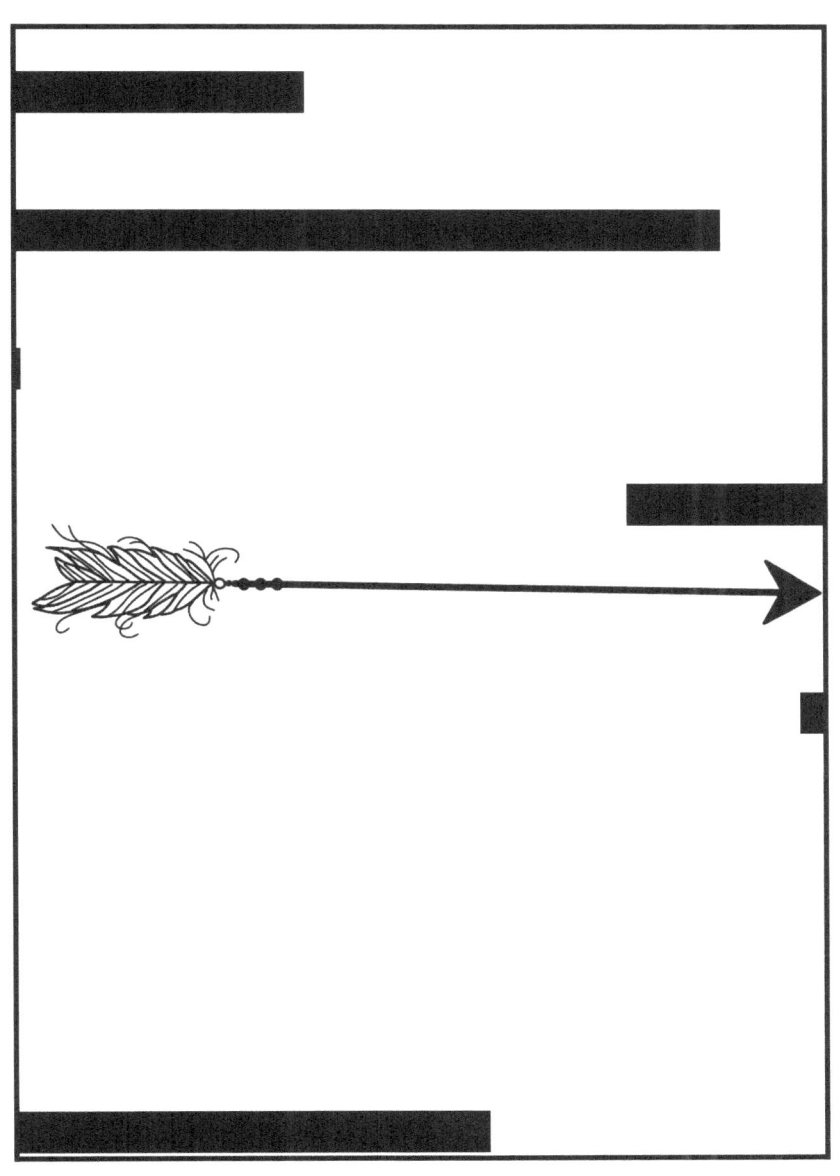

Chapter Sixteen

Servant Leadership

Being a servant leader in your business, ministry, or personal life means you are actively choosing to put the needs of others before your own. In our desire to be more like Jesus, may we always remember His instruction to do as He has done.

Choose Your Target: Keep things simple and reduce the chance for overthrow. This section helps you pick one target to focus on each chapter and knock down the barriers in your way.

What areas do you feel you are an expert in? Make a list of all the areas you could confidently lead.

_____
_____
_____
_____
_____
_____
_____
_____
_____
_____
_____
_____
_____
_____
_____
_____
_____
_____
_____
_____
_____
_____
_____
_____
_____
_____
_____
_____
_____

Choose the five that excite you the most.

_____
_____
_____
_____
_____

Narrow it down to the top three. These should be areas that you are most passionate about.

1 _____
2 _____
3 _____

Spend a few days in prayer as you consider which one area to focus on right now.

What is the one area you chose and what do plan on starting?

_____
_____
_____
_____
_____
_____
_____
_____
_____
_____
_____
_____
_____
_____

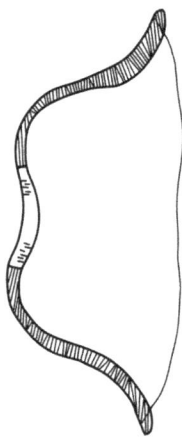

Raise Your Bow: You cannot shoot an arrow without a bow. This section helps you keep a list of tools and resources needed to help you hit your target.

Keep in mind the one area of focus you are ready to work on right now. What tools or resources do you need to begin leading?

_____

_____

_____

_____

_____

_____

_____

_____

_____

_____

_____

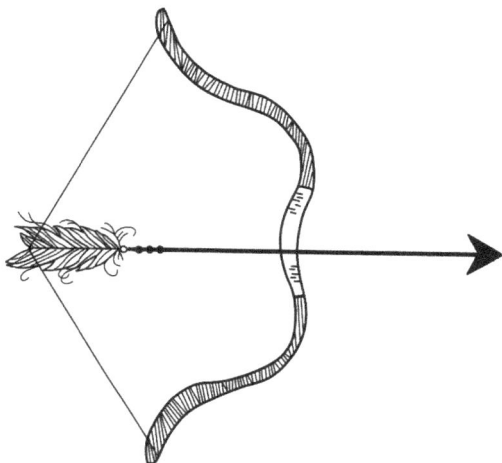

The Draw: Like pulling the bowstring back, this section takes a closer look at each chapter's pull quotes and the deeper lessons they hold.

Move forward with confidence, knowing you are now the one to instill hope in the lives of countless others as you honor God by fulfilling your calling.

What do you need to remind yourself you already know that gives you confidence in the direction you are going?

_____
_____
_____
_____
_____
_____
_____
_____
_____
_____
_____

What scripture best captures the feeling you want others to have when they walk away from working with you?

_____

_____

_____

_____

_____

_____

_____

_____

_____

_____

_____

_____

How do you feel now, knowing where God is calling you and having the confidence to answer His call by taking action now?

_____

_____

_____

_____

_____

_____

_____

_____

_____

_____

_____

_____

Centered Aim: If you want to hit the bullseye, center your aim. This section recaps the chapter's scripture and prayer.

> *"Am I now trying to win the approval of human beings, or of God? Or am I trying to please people? If I were still trying to please people, I would not be a servant of Christ."*
> Galatians 1:10

> *"Now that I, your Lord and Teacher, have washed your feet, you also should wash one another's feet. I have set you an example that you should do as I have done for you."*
> John 13:14-15

Prayer:
> *Father, I am so sorry for pleasing people instead of pleasing you. Help me let go of the need to be first and help me become last as I serve others. Please forgive me for not seeking You first, as I planned out my transition to becoming a servant leader. I hope to be a shining light so others may find you. Amen.*

Follow Through: To prevent premature dropping of the bow arm, a strong archer maintains their form after release. This section is a space for you to plan and track your steps.

You are ready. What are you going to build as you answer your call to become a servant leader?

_____
_____
_____
_____
_____
_____
_____
_____
_____
_____
_____
_____

What steps do you need to take to start now?

_____

_____

_____

_____

_____

_____

_____

_____

_____

_____

_____

_____

_____

_____

_____

_____

_____

_____

_____

_____

_____

_____

What is the deadline to complete this?

_____

_____

_____

After completing this section, add the steps needed as tasks in your to-do list.
Set important dates and reminders to stay on target for your deadline date.

A Letter from Shonda

Friend, you did it. Take a moment to let it sink in. When you first opened this journal, you may have been unsure what your calling was or where God was trying to take you. It is my prayer that now, upon completion of this journal, you not only have these answers, but you have a roadmap guiding you where to get started.

Each chapter, I had you pick one area to start and focus on despite choosing more than one to pick from. After you have implemented each area from each chapter, you can then go back and pick another, and another, and another. The beautiful thing about this journal is, you just created ideas for content, offerings, and services to incorporate as you grow.

Nothing is standing in your way of fulfilling your calling. You have everything you need and more!

It is my hope and prayer that as you become a servant leader in your area of expertise, you never lose sight of God's goodness through it all. You are doing Kingdom work!

I'd love to hear what you uncovered throughout this process. You can reach me via my website at www.shondaramsey.com or on any of my social channels. If you'd like to continue learning from me, be sure to sign up for my weekly newsletter on my website. It's a direct connection to me in your inbox.

I wish you nothing but success in all that you do.

With Grace,
Shonda Ramsey

www.ingramcontent.com/pod-product-compliance
Lightning Source LLC
Chambersburg PA
CBHW051618120626
46551CB00014B/1853